BILLY REED

Happy Derby!
Billy Reed

My Favorite Derby Stories

BUTLER BOOKS
LOUISVILLE

Butler Books
P.O. Box 7311
Louisville, KY 40207

ISBN 0-884532-48-9

Printed in Canada

CONTENTS

PREFACE

Has it been forty years? It seems as if it's been only the blink of an eye since I first met Billy Reed. Only yesterday, it seems, he was an enterprising young journalist, not the elder sports statesman he has become. Now, young writers and broadcasters seek him out for information on Kentucky sports, past and present.

Billy was a high school student, as was I, when his byline began to appear in the *Lexington Herald*. He was covering prep sports, writing about his fellow students, which I'm sure led to some interesting conversations at school after a big game loss.

After graduating from Transylvania University, Billy landed a job with the Louisville *Courier-Journal*, earning a national reputation with his ability to craft a story. However, Billy was not merely a wordsmith, he also became known for his aggressive investigative work. He would seek out a story, be it controversial or merely interesting. These were the qualities that earned Billy a columnist's role at the *Courier* and would carry his byline to the pages of *Sports Illustrated*.

Meanwhile, I had planned a career in thoroughbred racing and breeding, but took an unexpected turn into sports media, first with WVLK radio, then WLEX-TV in Lexington. In my new media role, Billy and I would often cover the same events. While involved in the coverage of all sports, I maintained my ties to the thoroughbred world as the announcer at the Keeneland Sales and later joined NBC as host of the Breeders' Cup. Like Billy, I have been lucky enough to reach a national audience while living in Kentucky. Through it all, Billy and I have shared many a laugh, many a spirited argument, but always with mutual respect.

I always thought that some of Billy's best work involved writing about thoroughbred racing. He was like a frisky foal, finally let loose to run at will and to explore interesting things. As Kentuckians, Billy and I have always shared a great interest in the Kentucky Derby. It is one of the world's most fascinating sporting events and not just for the two minutes of action on the track. The Derby is a mother lode of engaging stories, both equine and human, a bonanza for writers and broadcasters.

In 1968, Billy's investigation and reporting of the controversy surrounding Dancer's Image led to the only disqualification of a winner in Derby history. With the late Jim Bolus, then with the *Courier-Journal*, Billy wrote of the mysterious events leading up to race day, the subsequent investigation, and the eventual disqualification of Dancer's Image. The gray colt was removed as the Derby winner because of the presence of butazoladin in his system, a drug that, ironically, is now legal in most states.

In the aftermath of the Dancer's Image investigation I, too, had a minor coup. While working for WVLK radio in Lexington, I interviewed Mrs. Gene Markey, the owner of famed Calumet Farm. Calumet's Forward Pass had finished second to Dancer's Image in the 1968 Derby. In the interview, Mrs. Markey made news by declaring she would never race in Kentucky again if Forward Pass was not declared the official winner of the Derby, which is exactly what happened.

This work on the 1968 race cemented Billy Reed's credentials as both reporter and writer, and made him a recognized authority on thoroughbred racing. However, stories of scandal are the exception in Billy's writings of the Kentucky Derby. Most of his Derby stories are filled with joy and appreciation of being part of the whole scene of the "Run for the Roses." Billy describes the power and excitement of a Derby week workout shortly after dawn at Churchill Downs. He captures the optimism inherent in all the owners and trainers as the big day approaches, and makes the reader feel a part of the unfolding pageant.

In 2001, I realized a lifelong dream by hosting the Kentucky Derby on NBC. Billy has been living his dream of writing about the Derby for years. Now, at the point in our careers where dream and memory begin to merge, reflection is more frequent. This collection of Billy Reed's favorite columns on the Kentucky Derby remind me of how much this race means to me. I hope you enjoy them as much as I have.

—*Tom Hammond*

INTRODUCTION

It's admittedly presumptuous to do a book about your favorite Kentucky Derby stories because that implies that you think your work is somehow unique and better than others. I don't think that. My work pales in comparison with Joe Palmer, Damon Runyon, Red Smith, Jim Murray, Dave Kindred and so many other legendary sports writers who always made it a point to be in the Churchill Downs pressbox on the first Saturday in May.

Left to right: Jim Bolus, Dave Kindred, and Tom Callahan join Billy Reed at Churchill Downs.

My defense, then, must be rooted in longevity, volume and passion. I've loved the Derby longer than almost anybody still working, and I've written so much about it that I wanted to leave something, between hard covers, that my daughters, Amy and Susan, can hand their children if they ever ask, "So what was Grandad Reed's favorite sporting event?"

Like most boys born and reared in Kentucky, I grew up with an affinity for baseball, football, and, of course, basketball. I suppose the first time the Derby dented my consciousness was in 1953, when Dark Star shocked Native Dancer a couple of months before my 10th birthday. But it wasn't until 1964, when I was a junior at Transylvania University, that I really became interested in writing about thoroughbred racing in general and the Derby in particular.

At the time, J.B. Faulconer was both Keeneland's director of publicity and a general in the 100th Division of the U.S. Army Reserve Corps. One day, out of the goodness of his heart, J.B. took me aside and said, "Look, if you're going to be a sports writer in Kentucky, you really need to be able to write about thoroughbred racing." I respected J.B. so much that I immediately began trying to learn about the game, its people, and its legends.

It was, simply, the best advice I've ever received, which I pointed out when I delivered a eulogy for J.B. at his funeral in December, 2000.

In the 39 years since J.B. took me under his wing, I've learned that thoroughbred racing, more than any other sport, is a writer's dream. If you work the stable area at Churchill Downs the week before the Derby and can't find two or three fascinating tales to tell, then you're in the wrong business. From the lowliest groom to the wealthiest owner, everyone has a story to tell, usually a colorful one. And, unlike the major professional "ball" sports, the sources all are accessible and accommodating because of a shared desire to promote their unique sport.

When I began covering racing, I received a lot of help from J.B. and others, but the writer who was kindest to me also was the biggest name in the business: Joe Hirsch of *The Daily Racing Form*. No matter how busy he was, Joe always took the time to answer my questions and introduce me to somebody I needed to interview. As I've gotten older, I've tried hard to repay Joe by doing whatever I can to make newcomers feel welcome.

Billy Reed with Joe Hirsch in 1993 at Pimlico.

The other thing that makes racing special, from my perspective, is that no other sport has enabled me to establish so many long and lasting friendships. Some are mentioned in this book. But there are many others — you know who you are — who have allowed me to be a part of their personal lives, and vice-versa.

Should I apologize for this? Have my friendships compromised my integrity as a journalist? I hope not. Just as racing people always put the horse first, I've tried to put the reader first. It's not up to me to determine how successful I've been.

When many of my friends are represented in the Derby, I'm conflicted. I wish the best for each because I know how much it means to them and how hard they've worked. I empathize with what my friend, D. Wayne Lukas, experienced in the 1999 Derby. At the top of the stretch, the leader was Cat Thief, a colt that Lukas trained for William T. Young's Overbrook Farm. But in the final 16th, Cat Thief was overtaken and defeated by Charismatic, the colt Lukas trained for Bob and Beverly Lewis. At the same moment, Lukas had to be both elated and disappointed. He must have pulled it off, because both still have horses with him.

Billy Reed with daughters Amy and Susan at Churchill Downs.

I'm not a racetracker in the sense that I live the game 365 days a year. I'm interested in other sports and walks of life. But I am a racetracker in the sense that writing about the sport always has been one of my priorities. Believe it or not, I was the first sports editor of *The Courier-Journal* to cover the major Derby prep races and every Triple Crown race, every year. There was even a time when I passed up a World Series baseball game between the Yankees and Dodgers to cover the Jockey Club Gold Cup at Belmont Park.

"Reed," said my friend Dave Kindred, upon learning of my whereabouts, "you're crazy."

But Mike Barry and Jim Bolus understood perfectly. We were the "Three Amigos" who covered many races together. Jim and I both relied on Mike's experience—he saw his first Derby in 1922—but we didn't always agree with his opinions. But that was fine with Mike, a stubborn Irishman who loved a good argument as much as he loved a cold beer. To this day I miss them both enormously.

Mike Barry and Billy Red.

So for my daughters and Caroline Ruth and any future grandchildren with whom I may be blessed, this book is for you. I hope you'll always love thoroughbred racing and the Kentucky Derby. And never feel embarrassed about shedding a tear or two when "My Old Kentucky Home" is played at Churchill Downs on the first Saturday in May. I wouldn't have it any other way.

—Billy Reed

COL. MATT WINN
"Mr. Kentucky Derby"

[From the Kentucky Derby program, 2003]

It's interesting to consider if there would be a place in today's corporate world for Col. Matt Winn, the impresario who single-handedly promoted the Kentucky Derby into the world's best-known thoroughbred race. Once a tailor, he was too pudgy to look good in a suit. He also loved to chomp on cigars, a habit that would get him evicted from most areas of today's Churchill Downs.

But Winn was so charming and disarming that a friend once called him "The only Irish diplomat in existence." He also had the vision necessary to build the Derby, which was little more than a provincial race when Winn became the embodiment of Churchill's spirit 100 years ago this spring, into what sports writers came to call "the fastest two minutes in sports," or, more poetically, "The Run for the Roses."

Another sporting event, baseball's World Series, made its debut in 1903 and grew apace with the Derby until, at the time of Winn's death in 1949, the Series and the Derby, along with heavyweight championship fights and the Rose Bowl football game, were easily the nation's most popular spectator sports events. How did he do it? How did he turn a horse race in Louisville into an American institution?

By promoting the Derby 365 days a year. By being lucky. By keeping the Derby alive in spite of World Wars, the Great Depression, floods, and various reform movements designed to deprive Americans of their right to wager and consume alcohol. By ingratiating himself with the big-time owners and trainers in the East. By wining and dining the New York newspaper columnists, who were as influential then as network TV commentators are today.

Mostly, by being Matt Winn.

"Col. Winn's personality enabled him to walk with titans," former Churchill Downs publicity chief Brownie Leach once wrote. "He numbered among his close friends outstanding men in finance, industry, commerce, politics, and the professions. It was obvious they enjoyed his company and respected his judgment."

The son of a Louisville grocer, Winn was born on June 20, 1861, making him almost 14 when he saw the first Kentucky Derby in 1875 while standing in his father's grocery wagon in the "free parking" area of the infield.

He left St. Xavier High School shortly thereafter to become a bookkeeper, then a traveling salesman, and then a tailor. He maintained thoroughbred racing as one of his diversions. As legend has it, he once bet $5 each on two winning 100-to-l shots on the same afternoon in 1897.

Late in the autumn of 1902, former Downs official Charley Price dropped into Winn's office and urged him to do something to save Churchill, which was ready to fold due to poor management.

"I've been all over town trying to get a buyer," Price said. "No one wants it. I'm trying you as a last resort. Buy it and keep the Derby alive. If you don't, the Derby dies."

Apprehensive first, Winn eventually put together a group of investors who bought the track for $40,000 and named him vice-president. Under Winn's guidance, the track showed a profit in 1903 for the first time in years.

The investors convinced Winn to sell his tailoring business and become Churchill's full-time general manager, even though he had no experience in track management and would force himself to give up his personal interests as a gambler.

"It's simply my creed that an executive of a race track might bring certain censure upon the sport by owning horses that campaign at his track, or by betting on the outcome of races at a track where he is the supervisor," Winn said.

In 1908, Winn saved the Derby from reformers by reviving parimutuel wagering to replace conniving bookmakers. Then, in the years immediately before America entered World War I, the Derby was blessed by a series of fortuitous events that greatly enhanced its image.

Gamblers perked up when Donerail won the 1913 Derby and paid a record $184.90 for a $2 win wager. Racing purists were impressed that Old Rosebud broke the track record while winning the 1914 Derby. And females everywhere were thrilled when Harry Payne Whitney's Regret became the first filly to win the Derby in 1915.

Winn made certain that these novel stories received maximum national exposure, especially Whitney's remark that "this is the greatest race in America at the present time, and I don't care whether she (Regret) ever starts again. The glory of winning this event is big enough."

Ever the promoter, Winn kept the Derby alive during World War I by growing carnations in the infield and selling them for the benefit of the Red Cross.

By 1918, Winn was such a big name in racing that he began lending his expertise to tracks such as Douglas Park, Empire City, Crescent City, City Park, Lincoln Fields, Washington Park, Laurel Park, Latonia, Lexington, Fairmount Park, Juarez, and Mexico City. These jobs expanded his influence and enabled him to promote the Kentucky Derby on a daily basis.

The Derby's image was further enhanced in 1922, when the Derby and Preakness were held the same day. Both wanted Morvich, the undefeated 2-year-old champion of the previous year, but Winn prevailed by twisting the arm of Ben Block, the Wall Street financier who owned Morvich.

Naturally, the New York press followed Morvich and reported his victory in glowing terms. Four New York papers—the *Times*, the *Morning Telegraph*, the *Tribune*, and the *World*—put the story of Morvich's victory on page one.

From then on, the Derby's prestige, purse, and attendance grew steadily, thanks to Winn's constant prodding. He established his off-season base in New York City, at the Waldorf-Astoria Towers, and entertained the columnists whose by-lines were known from coast-to-coast—Bill Corum, Damon Runyon, Grantland Rice, and others.

The writers fell in love with Winn, knowing they could always turn to him for a fresh quote or a free drink. He never let a newspaper guy pick up a check because, as Winn liked to put it, "Give me the five best writers in New York, and you can have the rest."

One of those five was Arthur Daley of *The New York Times*. "He could give cards and spades to Barnum and beat him," Daley wrote. "The Kentucky Derby is a monument to him. It's his baby, and his alone. He will always be a part of it, even more a part of it than the spired towers at Churchill Downs."

Oscar Otis of *The Daily Racing Form* agreed. "Winn was always personally available to the press," Otis said. "He liked newspapermen, was witty, treated them like kings, and gave them the run of the backstretch to do their own news digging. Moreover, he was a rather courtly and distinguished personality, but he did not have a trace of snobbery in him."

During World War II, when the government imposed a travel embargo that threatened to kill the Derby, Winn declared solemnly that "the Derby will be held even if there is only one starter and the only spectators are the trainer, owner, and myself."

He worked out a compromise with the government by asking that out-of-town Derby patrons turn over their tickets, for the duration, to GIs stationed near Louisville. Thus, the 1943 and '44 classics were called the "Streetcar Derbys" because most of the crowd lived close enough to ride streetcars to Churchill Downs.

From the 1920s until his death in 1949, Winn lived in a six-room apartment at the track, where he always entertained the Derby winners and many of his friends. In the off-season, he often could be seen wandering around the track, followed by a valet carrying a cane-bottom chair. Sometimes he would stop and sit to study the track's gardens and grandstands, looking for ways to improve them.

"He lived the Derby 24 hours a day," said *Courier-Journal* turf writer Jerry McNerney. "He ate with it, slept with it, and talked about it to anybody willing to listen."

One thing Winn never did was announce the actual Derby Day attendance, saying only that it was "more than 100,000." He felt that, if the attendance dropped one year due to bad weather or some other misfortune, the public might get the idea that the Derby was slipping. And that was simply unacceptable.

Winn ran his Derby attendance streak to 75 in a row when he watched Calumet Farm's Ponder win the Diamond Jubilee Derby in 1949. He was 88 when he died on October 6 of that year, the same day that Preacher Roe of the Brooklyn Dodgers was pitching his team to a 2-1 victory over the New York Yankees in Yankee Stadium, tying the Series at a game each.

From New York, Winn's old friend Runyon wrote a touching farewell. "I have known a great many men in sport in my time," he typed. "I have known the champions and the promoters. I have known the magnates and the moguls. I have known those who could take the good and the bad with the same kind of smile, and I have known crybabies—the ones who could not stand up when the going got tough. But of them all, I have never known one who has worn as well as Colonel Winn."

Any modern executive would love to have that as an epitaph.

JOHN D. HERTZ
"Want A Winner, Mr. Capone?"

[From the Churchill Downs Website, November 2002]

The 1928 Derby Winner, Reigh Count, found himself right in the middle of a frightening battle between his owner, rental-car magnate John D. Hertz, and Alphonse "Scarface Al" Capone, who was making an estimated $20 million a year as Chicago's No. 1 gangster.

In the colt's 2-year-old season in 1927, the nation was percolating from a vibrant sports year in which Babe Ruth hit an astounding 60 home runs for the New York Yankees, Gene Tunney had defended his heavyweight boxing championship against Jack Dempsey in the infamous "long count" fight in Chicago, and golfer Bobby Jones won both the British Open and U.S. Amateur championships.

That also was the year that Arlington Park opened in Chicago. Built by H.D. "Curley" Brown and his associates, the track was in financial trouble from the moment it opened its gates on October 13, 1927. When word got around that a group fronting for Capone might try to buy the track, Hertz vowed that he wouldn't let it happen.

But Chicago wasn't on Hertz's mind when he and trainer B.S. Mitchell sent the high-strung Reigh Count to the post in the Kentucky Jockey Club. Hertz, who had finished fifth in the 1923 Kentucky Derby with Chittagong, was looking for a horse that could take him to the winner's circle on Derby Day, 1928.

Hertz had bought Reigh Count from William S. Kilmer of Virginia

Mr. and Mrs. John D. Hertz with Count Fleet.

after watching him try to "savage," or bite, a rival during a maiden race in August at Saratoga. Kilmer was happy to sell because he was convinced that Sun Beau, another of his 2-year-olds, was far better than the temperamental Reigh Count.

Under jockey Chick Lang, whose son and namesake later would become the general manager at Pimlico, Reigh Count won the Kentucky Jockey Club. However, his record as a 2-year-old (four wins and three seconds in 14 starts) hardly stamped him as the favorite for the 1928 Kentucky Derby.

Nevertheless, he matured over the winter and looked so impressive in the spring that he and stablemate Reigh Olga (owned by Hertz associate Otto Lehman) were made the $2.06-to-$1 favorite in the 22-horse Derby field.

The '28 Derby was held on Saturday, May 19, eight days after Victorian had won the Preakness in Baltimore. But Reigh Count didn't run in the Preakness and Victorian didn't come to Louisville. Under Lang, Reigh Count settled into fifth in the early going, moved up to press the leaders at the top of the stretch, and took the lead at the eighth pole to draw off for a three-length victory over Misstep.

One of Hertz's guests at the Derby was Warren Wright, owner of the Calumet Baking Soda empire. Reigh Count's victory got him hooked on racing, and a few years later he established Calumet Farm. When Wright began buying horses for breeding purposes, Hertz suggested Nellie Morse, the filly who had won the 1924 Preakness.

In foal to American Flag, she gave birth to a filly, Nellie Flag, who won the 1934 Kentucky Jockey Club and became the first thoroughbred champion to carry Wright's Calumet colors of devil's red and blue. The farm's eight Derby winners from 1941 through '68 still are a record.

But back to Reigh Count. Because Hertz wanted to have a fresh horse for the major fall races in New York, Reigh Count didn't run in the Belmont Stakes, which was won by Vito, a colt who had finished second to Reigh Count in the '27 Kentucky Jockey Club and 20th behind him in the '28 Derby. But then came the shadow of Capone.

At Saratoga in August of '28, oil-soaked rags and pools of oil were found in the Hertz barn, where Reigh Count and Anita Peabody, who had defeated her male stablemate in the previous year's Futurity, were stabled.

And less than two months later, a fire broke out in Reigh Count's barn at Hertz's Leona Stock Farm near Cary, Illinois. Reigh Count was saved, but 11 horses worth an estimated $225,000 perished in the flames, including a half-sister to Anita Peabody. Arson investigators discovered oil-soaked material in the ruins. Also in October, Hertz received enough death threats to force him to hire a bodyguard, and a kidnap threat that made him send his only grandchild out of Illinois. For years to come, Hertz refused to sit near a car window, apparently because he feared being shot.

Naturally, the prime suspect was Capone, who still had designs on Arlington Park. However, there was no proof that directly linked the Capone mob to the fires or the threats.

In January of 1929, as Reigh Count was getting ready for his 4-year-old season, Hertz disposed of most of his holdings in Yellow Cab and retired as chairman of the board. At roughly the same time, he raised $2.5 million in 18 minutes to buy Arlington Park from the Brown group and save the 1,000-acre property from the gangsters.

Hertz put up $666,000 of his own money, then solicited Albert D. Lusskey, an advertising magnate, and William Wrigley, whose family owned the chewing-gum company and the Chicago Cubs, to put up $110,000 each. Incorporated as the Arlington Jockey Club, the new owners appointed Otto Lehman president and Charles McCulloch, head of worldwide operations for the Yellow Cab Company, as chairman of the board.

"Public opinion was outraged at the prospect of hoodlums dominating racing in Chicago," Hertz said.

In 1931, Capone was convicted of income-tax evasion and sent to prison, where he died in 1947. The Hertz group owned Arlington until April 16, 1940,

Count Fleet wins the Kentucky Derby, 1943. Note the sign: "In case of air raid keep calm."

when it sold to John D. Allen, vice-president of Brinks & Co., and Benjamin F. Lindheimer, a director of Washington Park, for "exactly the sum, down to the nickel, that its rescuers had put in," said Hertz.

From the Yellow Cab Company, Hertz spun off a business that became Hertz Rental Cars. He also was a partner in Lehman Bros., the Wall Street investment banking firm, and a director of corporations involved in transportation, oil, sports, and movies.

After Reigh Count won the Coronation Cup in 1929, Hertz shipped him to England, where he finished second in the Ascot Gold Cup and went unplaced in three handicaps. He then was retired to stud at Hertz's farm in Cary, Illinois, but was moved to Claiborne Farm in Kentucky in 1936 because Hertz finally conceded that the location and climate were not good for breeding purposes.

A.B. Hancock, Sr., the boss at Claiborne, told Hertz he should buy some adjoining farmland and start his own breeding farm. That's how it came to be that in 1939, Hertz opened the Stoner Creek Farm and moved Reigh Count there.

On March 24, 1940, the mare Quickly gave birth to a son of Reigh Count at Stoner Creek. Named Count Fleet, the colt was available to be purchased for $4,500. But when he got no takers, Hertz kept him to run, as he did Reigh Count, in his wife Fanny's name and his black-and-gold silks.

In 1943, Count Fleet won racing's Triple Crown. And when one of his sons, Count Turf, won the 1951 Kentucky Derby, it was the first time the "Run for the Roses" had been captured by three generations of the same sire line.

In reality, the Kentucky Jockey Club, now sponsored by Brown & Williamson, hasn't proved to be a good precursor of the next year's Derby winner. After Reigh Count's Jockey Club-Derby double, Clyde Van Dusen duplicated the feat in 1928-'29 and Gallant Fox did it in 1930-'31. But in the last 71 years, only Cannonade in 1973-'74 has turned the trick.

In 1997-'98, Real Quiet, owned by Mike Pegram and trained by Bob Baffert, came close, finishing third in the Kentucky Jockey Club, but coming back to win the next year's Derby as the "silent partner" of the ballyhooed Indian Charlie.

The 75th anniversary of Reigh Count's win in the Kentucky Derby won't be won by a colt owned by a rental-car magnate who's in the front trenches of the battle against organized crime.

But maybe he'll be good enough to wake up the ghost of Reigh Count, wherever it's lurking under the Twin Spires, and go on to achieve the same kind of immortality enjoyed by Reigh Count, Count Fleet, and Count Turf.

THE FIGHTING FINISH
Did the Right Horse Win?

[From *The Courier-Journal*, April 1983]

In Hollywood, Florida, a palmy little suburb north of Miami, the leading characters in the most famous of all Kentucky Derbies are still forced to talk and think about their historic duel at Churchill Downs on the afternoon of May 6, 1933. They live only a mile or so apart, but they are inexorably side-by-side in the public's memory. Although neither Don Meade nor Herb Fisher could have known it at the time, their lives were forever changed by what happened in a few scant seconds of old-fashioned, roughhouse race-riding that produced what history has come to identify as the "Fighting Finish."

That was the Derby in which Meade, aboard Brokers Tip, outdueled Fisher, on Head Play, to the finish by a nose.

Or did he?

Now 71, Fisher still contends that his colt was the winner. Those were the days, remember, before the film patrol and the photo-finish camera. And Fisher says that three of the four stewards told him that Head Play, not Brokers Tip, won the 59th Derby.

But the chief steward, Charles Price, overruled his colleagues and Fisher's claim of foul. He let Brokers Tip stand as the winner. The reason, Fisher believes, was that Brokers Tip was owned by the Idle Hour Stock Farm of the famed Col. E. R. Bradley.

"Bradley was the king of Kentucky in those days," said Fisher one spring morning in a 1983 interview at his home. "Gave hundreds of thousands to charity. No way they (the stewards) weren't going to give it to him. If that had been me on his horse, I'd have won it."

Only an hour earlier, sitting in his home, Meade, now 69, had told another story. Asked if he had won the race, Meade said, "No question about it—and by more than a nose, too."

And so, in a way, the 1933 Derby isn't finished—and the two riders still are fighting. Oh, they claim to be friends now, but it took them 25 years after the '33 Derby to shake hands and make up. Still, their accounts of the race that made them famous differ remarkably.

In the absence of a photo of the finish, the only clue to what happened is perhaps the most famous photograph in sports history—certainly the most reprinted one ever taken by a photographer for *The Courier-Journal*. His name was Wallace Lowry, and on that fateful day, as the riders fought down the stretch, he was lying on the ground, just under the inner rail, only a few yards from the finish line.

Because he was using an old-fashioned graphic camera instead of the motor-driven 35mm models that today's photographers have, Lowry had only one shot at a photo. Remarkably, he got it—a stark, dramatic shot that shows Meade and Fisher holding on to each other as their horses thundered toward their destiny.

Don Meade signed a copy of the famous photo to Billy Reed.

The trouble is, it's impossible to tell who was ahead at that moment, much less who was ahead when the horses hit the finish.

In 1983, to celebrate the race's 50th anniversary, Meade and Fisher both were brought back to Louisville to relive the "Fighting Finish." Both were special guests of the Derby Festival Committee and its chairman, Dan Mangeot.

Both Meade, who operates a Hollywood bar, and Fisher, now retired, claim to be puzzled by the continuing fascination with what happened in the '33 Derby. They have told the story so many times—and now will have to tell it over and again when they return to the scene.

The facts are pretty clear about what happened until the stretch.

Head Play was such an ill-tempered, strong horse that he wouldn't go into the starting gate. He was allowed to break from outside the gate, and Fisher was able to get him off to a running start that enabled him to go to the lead after about six furlongs.

The track was so muddy that Meade kept Brokers Tip about 10 feet away from the rail. Going into the first turn, he had only one horse beaten in the 13-horse field, but Meade skillfully moved through and around horses until, at the top of the stretch, only Head Play and Charley O. were ahead.

According to Fisher, the rider on Charley O. drew next to him and yelled, "Watch the inside!" Sure enough, here came Meade, moving Brokers Tip to the rail and going for the lead.

Only 19 at the time, Meade was a cocky, fearless kid who was to become one of the sport's all-time great riders. He would be in racing's Hall of Fame today had he not gotten into so many scrapes with racing authorities that, in 1945, he was denied a license, bringing his career to a premature end.

Now, with Meade challenging on the inside, Fisher made the decision that proved to be his undoing. Instead of staying away and minding his own business, Fisher moved Head Play to the left, toward Brokers Tip, in an attempt to intimidate Meade and shut him off.

Meade: "When he saw me coming at the head of the stretch, he beared in on me, and I just pushed him off."

Fisher: "I just wanted to tighten up on him. I just squeezed him against the fence, and he grabbed ahold of the saddlecloth. I didn't know he had ahold of me until a sixteenth of a mile from the finish."

Meade: "He grabbed ahold of me, and we grabbed, grabbed, grabbed all through the stretch. It was a survival of the fittest. I'm not blaming him for what he did, because in those days that's what you did. It was an accepted thing."

Fisher: "I hit him across the head with my whip once or twice before the finish and once after. He switched his hold from the saddlecloth to my left shoulder and all but pulled the reins out of my hands. He was holding on to me, and I was pulling him."

Meade: "He hit me with the whip after the finish, but not before. His reins were dangling perhaps the last sixteenth of a mile. If he'd just ridden his horse, he'd have won by two or three lengths."

Fisher: "I know I rode the best horse and should have won it. He grabbed ahold of me for an eighth of a mile, and my horse drug him another eighth."

The winning margin was listed as the scantest of margins—a nose. Fisher contends that, in such cases, the naked eye always favors the inside horse— Brokers Tip, in this case. He also contends that he would have won the race had Brokers Tip been owned by anybody other than Col. Bradley.

Over the years more has been made of the duel than was made at the time. Both Fisher and Meade blame the *C-J* photograph. Said Meade, "Had it not been for that picture, the whole thing would have been forgotten."

At the time, after hitting Meade with his whip as soon as they crossed the finish line, Fisher broke into tears when the decision was announced, then attacked Meade in a jocks' room fight broken up by *C-J* reporter John Herchenroeder, who was eventually to become the paper's city editor and its first ombudsman.

Now, though, Fisher claims he's glad that it happened the way it did because, by finishing second in such a controversial race, he has received more attention over the years than a lot of jockeys who won the Derby.

"It used to be that I'd walk into a bar and order a drink only to have three sitting in front of me before I knew it," Fisher said. "Once or twice I got mad. I had a pretty good training career, and all people wanted to talk about was that Derby."

And that's all they talked about when the old-timers came to Louisville in 1983 to celebrate the 50th anniversary of the most famous Derby of all. It was their last hurrah, because both died within the next few years.

SILKY SULLIVAN
The Derby's First TV Idol

[From the Churchill Downs Website, April 2000]

"And now here comes Silky Sullivan!"

When the track announcer made that announcement during the 1958 Santa Anita Derby, the then-record crowd of 61,123 that showed up for California's main Kentucky Derby prep race began to scream and stomp for the big, handsome chestnut who had captured their hearts with his come-from-way-behind running style.

Silky Sullivan was more than just a racehorse. He was a phenomenon, the star of his own TV show and ghost-written newspaper column. He was the "people's horse," a Hollywood matinee idol with a flair for drama and suspense. Just when he seemed hopelessly beaten, he actually had the opposition right where he wanted them.

The Santa Anita Derby was vintage Silky. In the first five furlongs, he fell 28 lengths off the pace. But when jockey Bill Shoemaker rattled his bit—Silky didn't like to get hit with the whip—here he came, flying past horses until he was 3-1/2 lengths ahead at the finish line.

"We vow faithfully to write of Silky Sullivan as if he were a horse," the *Thoroughbred of California* told its readers. "Which, of course, is ridiculous."

In the 44 years since Silky became a cultural icon, the Santa Anita Derby has produced 10 Derby winners. Of those, there was a Triple Crown winner (Affirmed in '78), a filly (Winning Colors in '88), four Horses of the Year (Affirmed twice, Ferdinand in '87, Sunday Silence in '89, Charismatic in '99), and two colts who had Triple Crowns snatched away in the final strides of the Belmont Stakes (Silver Charm in '97 and Real Quiet in '98).

Yet none of them mesmerized the public quite like Silky Sullivan. As a 2-year-old, he drew attention to himself by coming from 27 lengths off the pace to win the Golden Gate Futurity. The next year, he came from 40 lengths out of it to lose by a neck to Old Pueblo in the California Breeders' Champion Stakes. In his next start, he came from 41 lengths behind to win a 6-1/2-furlong allowance race.

No wonder co-owner Tom Ross's doctors didn't let him watch Silky's races because of his heart problems. Ross and Phil Klipstein bought Silky for $10,700 in 1956 at Del Mar. The name came from his breeding, by Sullivan out of Lady N Silk.

After the Santa Anita Derby, trainer Reggie Cornell honored a commitment to send Silky to Golden Gate Fields, where it rained so hard every day that Cornell wasn't able to train Silky the way he wanted or keep him in top condition. Sent off as the 3-to-10 favorite in a mile allowance race, the overweight Silky was only third, disappointing the record weekday crowd of 19,012. "Silky needed that race real bad," Cornell growled.

Then it was on to Louisville, where the drugstores were selling Silky Sundaes and the bars were offering Irish whisky drinks named after him. The Saturday before the Derby, Cornell entered Silky in the seven-furlong Steppingstone Purse at Churchill Downs. Despite an afternoon rain, a huge crowd turned out to see Silky in the flesh.

Typically, he dropped back by 32 lengths in the early going. When he finally made his run, he began passing horses as if they were standing still. At the end, he was fourth, beaten only 2-1/2 lengths. One clocker had him running the last eighth of a mile in a sizzling 10-2/5 seconds.

"They'll never beat this horse in the Derby," Shoemaker said.

The week before the race, Silky made the covers of *Time* and *Sports Illustrated*. An estimated 4,000 fans visited his barn, not counting reporters and photographers. So huge was his popularity that Western Union reported its press file was 40 percent higher than any previous Derby.

On May 3, 1958, the track was muddy for the Derby due to week-long rains. Although Silky didn't much care for the mud, his backers in the crowd of 70,451 bought a record number of $2 win tickets on him. Many planned on keeping them as souvenirs instead of cashing them. At post time, there almost was a tri-favorite. The entry of Jewel's Reward and Ebony Pearl were sent off at 2-1, with Silky and Calumet Farm's Tim Tam tied for second choice at $2.10-to-1.

Soon after starter James Thomson released the field of 14, Silky dropped 32 lengths behind the pace-setting Lincoln Road. But CBS, who had the Derby rights in those days, was ready. For the first time, the network used a split screen, all the better to keep an eye on Silky. Unfortunately for the network and Silky's many fans, the "California Comet" never got going and beat only two horses.

He finished some 20 lengths behind the victorious Tim Tam, who was a half-length better than second-place Lincoln Road. "Never," said racing historian Jim Bolus, "has any horse received so much fanfare and run so poorly."

Silky also got more attention than any 12th-place finisher in Derby history. Besides the split-screen, Fred Caposella, calling the race for CBS, mentioned Silky's name five times and Tim Tam's only once during the first mile and an eighth. At the end, the score was Silky 6, Tim Tam 4.

"All the publicity in the world couldn't have moved Silky up enough to win the Derby," Shoemaker said years later. "Silky wasn't a bad horse, but he wasn't really a good horse, either. He didn't have the class to run with the good horses. In California, he beat some mediocre horses and looked good doing it, but I said then that he couldn't spot a horse like Tim Tam 25 lengths and expect to beat him."

Which, of course, isn't even close to what he told Cornell after the Stepping Stone.

Sent on to the Preakness Stakes, Silky received another warm reception from his fans, but again was disappointing, finishing only eighth. He went back to California, and was retired after his 4-year-old season with 12 victories to show from 27 starts and career earnings of $157,700. As a breeding stallion, Silky also was a dud, producing only four stakes winners.

In retirement, Silky annually was brought to Golden Gate Fields for St. Patrick's Day and to Santa Anita for the Santa Anita Derby. In 1977, he was paraded at both those tracks before dying in November at age 22.

"It was fun while it lasted," said co-owner Ross, whose heart outlasted Silky's by only a month and a half.

In one sense, Silky was a bust, a flash-in-the-pan, a sucker horse. But in another, he was almost as good for racing as Man o' War, Citation, and Secretariat. He was horse racing's first hero of the TV age. He drew big crowds and even attracted the attention of many who previously had little, or no, interest in racing.

He even became a part of American slang. Anytime an athlete, a team, or a politician had to overcome a big deficit to win, they were said to be "doing a Silky Sullivan."

Fans still love a horse who comes from way off to win. In 2001, for example, Monarchos was 13th after a half mile, about 18 lengths behind the leader, before uncorking a monster move in the final turn to move into contention and gallop on to record the second fastest winning time in Derby history.

Still, Monarchos never lost contact with his field the way Silky did as a matter of routine. Once, Shoemaker said Silky got so far behind that he couldn't see the leaders—not because of dirt in his face but because they were so far ahead.

Naturally, Silky got up to win.

NORTHERN DANCER
The King of Sires

[Thoroughbred: Celebration of a Breed, January 1989]

On the afternoon of April 24, 1964, nobody at the Keeneland Association's race course in Lexington, Kentucky, could imagine that the favorite in the Blue Grass Stakes someday would send back sons and daughters to the association's sales pavilion that would rewrite the record books. In fact, after the way Northern Dancer performed, it was difficult even to envision what would happen nine days later against powerful Hill Rise in the 90th Kentucky Derby at Churchill Downs. But that has been the story of Northern Dancer's life. Always defying logic and the odds, always having to prove himself, always coming out with the last horse laugh. His success has been so overwhelming that it's possible to make the argument that no horse in modern history has had as much worldwide impact on the game.

The story of Northern Dancer begins with E. P. Taylor, master of the famed Windfields Farm of Willowdale, Ontario, Canada. He made his fortune as head of Argus Corporation, a holding company that included breweries, farm equipment firms and real estate. During World War II, Taylor was cited by the British and Canadian governments for extraordinary service to the empire as a buyer of essential materials. After the war, he became so involved in Canadian racing that, when tracks in the Toronto area fell into disrepair in the early 1950s, he bought them as head of Jockey Club, Ltd., and built two new tracks that gave Canadian racing a much-needed boost.

In 1960, Taylor sent to Churchill Downs a filly named Natalma to run

Northern Dancer, the pride of Canada, wins the 1964 Preakness.

in the Kentucky Oaks and a colt named Victoria Park to contest the Derby. His luck wasn't good. After Natalma came up with a bum knee and was scratched from the Oaks, Victoria Park ran third in the Derby won by Venetian Way. For a month afterward, Taylor's cosmopolitan trainer, Senor Horatio Luro, debated about whether to send Natalma back to the farm. When he finally did, she was bred to the sire Nearctic. The foal, born on May 27, 1961, was named Northern Dancer because of Natalma's sire, the great Native Dancer, and the farm's northerly location.

At that time it was Taylor's custom to put a price tag on almost every one of his yearlings. For Northern Dancer, who was on the small side, the asking price was $25,000. Nobody took him, although a wealthy Irishman took a serious look at him in the sales ring. So Taylor kept him and turned him over to Luro, which turned out to be an historic turn of events.

Luro was born in Buenos Aires on February 2, 1901. He was the fourth generation of a family of Argentine horsemen and cattlemen. It was inevitable that Luro would follow his father, Adolfo, into the family business. As a young man, Luro took up the various pastimes common to the well-bred. His family forced him to give up driving sports cars following a race in which his brother was killed. Says Luro, "My brother drove a Dusenberg, and it was too fast for the circuit."

After his father's death in 1937, Luro came to the United States hoping to pick up a lot of big purse money with horses bred in Argentina. He found his way to California, where his debonair manner, elegant breeding and proficiency at polo gained him entrance to the right Hollywood circles. One of his first clients was crooner Bing Crosby. One introduction led to another, and soon the dapper Luro was escorting some of Hollywood's most glamorous leading ladies, including Lana Turner, Ava Gardner and Loretta Young.

He began making a name for himself in U.S. breeding through Princequillo, a horse he claimed for $2,500 and turned into a distance champion. When it was time for Princequillo to be retired to stud, Luro sent him to A. B. "Bull" Hancock at the Claiborne Farm of Paris, Kentucky, and Princequillo turned out to be one of the cornerstones in the breeding dynasty Hancock was to build.

Because of his friendship with polo-playing buddy George Pope, Luro got a colt named Decidedly, who won the Kentucky Derby in 1962. That same year Pope, owner of El Peco Ranch, asked Luro to pick out a yearling to train for him. The next day the colt was vanned to Luro, but the trainer sent him back because "he is not the one I picked." That colt turned out to be Hill Rise, the first of several quirks of fate leading to the 1964 Derby.

Early in Northern Dancer's racing career, he was so feisty that Luro wanted to geld him, only to be overruled by Taylor. The reason was a horse named Roman Flair.

"Mr. Taylor had bought Roman Flair at Saratoga," Windfields vice-president Joe Thomas once told Maryjean Wall of the *Lexington Herald-Leader*. "'He was a mean, willful horse, so Luro convinced Mr. Taylor that if he was castrated, it would make a good horse out of him. So we castrated him, but before he got back to the races he bowed a tendon. Then he ran for $1,500 at Finger Lakes. When the question of Northern Dancer came up, Mr. Taylor said, 'If it didn't work before, why now?'" That decision, of course, was to alter the course of breeding history.

Perhaps because Luro had trained both Nearctic and Natalma, he could see things in little Northern Dancer that others couldn't. As a two-year-old in 1963, Northern Dancer had seven wins in nine starts, all in Canada except his two-length victory for jockey Manuel Ycaza in the mile Remsen on November 27 at New York's Aqueduct. In early December, the colt suffered a quartercrack that put him behind schedule for the Kentucky Derby heading into 1964.

Before the colt's three-year-old debut in a six-furlong race at Hialeah, Luro named Bobby Ussery to ride the colt and gave him specific orders to not whip Northern Dancer under any circumstances. However, after the colt got knocked sideways leaving the gate, Ussery rushed the colt into contention and began hitting him at the eighth pole. The colt finished only third, which left Luro furious.

"Two days later," Luro told Joe Hirsch of *The Daily Racing Form*,

E.P. Taylor, owner of Northern Dancer and the founder of the Jockey Club of Canada.

"Northern Dancer refused to go to the track. The Flamingo was coming along, and I had to do something, so I had him jogged every morning for a week, up and down the dirt path behind the barns. He knew he wasn't going to the track, so he relaxed and, at the end of a week's time, the whipping wasn't a problem for him."

With Bill Shoemaker replacing Ussery, Northern Dancer moved into serious Kentucky Derby contention with a two-length victory in Hialeah's Flamingo, followed by a length victory in the Florida Derby at Gulfstream. But then Shoemaker made one of the most famous decisions in racing history, taking off Northern Dancer to replace young Don Pierce about Hill Rise, the established class of the California runners. Luro immediately signed Bill Hartack, who had ridden Decidedly to victory for him in the 1962 Derby. Hartack also had sniffed the roses in 1957 with Iron Leige and in 1960 with Venetian Way. Asked about Shoemaker's decision, Luro said, "I'm not upset at all. I guess Shoemaker must not have been impressed with my horse's race Saturday (in the Florida Derby), but I believe it was far from his best effort and that he'll do better."

At Keeneland, both Hill Rise and Northern Dancer became acquainted with their new riders. After Hill Rise's three-quarters of a length victory in the seven-furlong Forerunner Purse on April 17, Shoemaker said the colt was "kinda lazy." But if Hill Rise wasn't impressive, neither was Northern Dancer in the Blue Grass. Sent off as the 1-5 favorite, the colt finished only a half-length ahead of Allen Adair. Nevertheless, Hartack seemed pleased. Since he wasn't talking to the press in those days, the writers had to be satisfied with an exchange that Hartack had with a program salesman on his way to the jocks' room.

"Hey, Bill," yelled the guy, "when did you think you had it?"

"When I got the mount," shot back a grinning Hartack.

The rider of Allen Adair, Jimmy Nichols, agreed. "He (Hartack) never turned him loose," Nichols said. "He did just a little when we ran up on him down the stretch, but then he just rapped him and he was gone."

Asked to evaluate his colt's performance, Luro smiled and made the statement that has become part of racing lore. "You do not squeeze the lemon dry," said Luro, by way of explaining that he wanted to be certain that Northern Dancer would have plenty of juice left for the Kentucky Derby.

In retrospect, Northern Dancer-Hill Rise was one of the finest duels in Derby history. Under a sensational ride by Hartack, the little colt drew away in the stretch turn, then had enough heart and courage to hold off Shoemaker's charge on Hill Rise. An historic photograph taken by Bill Strode of *The Courier-Journal* shows Hartack looking over his shoulder at Shoemaker near the finish. The winner's time of 2:00 for the mile and a quarter was a record that stood until Secretariat broke it in 1973.

Naturally, when it was over, Shoemaker was the object of almost as much second-guessing as he had been in 1957, when he misjudged the Derby finish line aboard Gallant Man and momentarily stood up in the irons, giving Hartack and Iron Leige the edge they needed to win. Said The Shoe, "I guess one of the reasons I picked Hill Rise was because you can get into him and go to riding. Northern Dancer is not a stick horse."

Unconvinced by the Derby, the public again made Hill Rise the favorite over Northern Dancer two weeks later in the Preakness. But this time the little tiger from Canada was even more superior, drawing away for a 2-1/4-length victory over The Scoundrel with Hill Rise third by a head. By now, even the skeptics had to be convinced that Northern Dancer was a good bet to become racing's first Triple Crown winner since Citation in 1948. Alas, however, the colt was only third in the Belmont, struggling home behind Quadrangle and Roman Brother. Only two weeks later, making his final start in Canada, Northern Dancer scored a resounding 7-1/2-length victory for Taylor, Luro and Hartack in the mile-and-a-quarter Queen's Plate at Woodbine in Toronto.

After Northern Dancer was retired to stud, Taylor received lots of advice about what to do with him. His old friend Bull Hancock said he could stand him at a farm in Kentucky. "What have you got up there in Canada?" Hancock said. "You've got ice and snow. There's no way you can breed a good horse there."

Nevertheless, during Northern Dancer's four seasons in Canada, he produced the colts that were to become the European champions Nijinsky II and The Minstrel. In December 1968, he was moved to the Maryland division of the Windfields operation.

"We wanted to continue to manage him," Thomas said. "He was still our horse. If we had sent him to Kentucky to one of the big farms there, they would have wanted to take over the management of him. We felt that Maryland was convenient enough that anybody that had a good mare in Kentucky or anyplace else would send her to Maryland because there wasn't the same resistance about being too far north.

In 1970, at the age of nine, Northern Dancer was syndicated for $2.4 million, or 32 shares for $75,000 each. In retrospect, that was one of the biggest bargains in the game's history. By the fall of 1981, Northern Dancer's impact on the breeding game already was so great that Windfields turned down an offer of $40 million for the stallion, then a ripe old 20.

At Keeneland, home of the world's most prestigious horse auction, Northern Dancer's blood became hotly coveted in the late 1970s because of his offsprings' success in the European classics. His two most famous offspring, Nijinksy II and The Minstrel, both winners of the Epsom Derby, also became great sires in their own right.

"One of the great qualities Northern Dancer had was his ability to accelerate," Thomas once told racing historian Jim Bolus. "In the Derby, he's just sitting in there and when the hole opened up, Hartack said go. He just stepped on it and was gone. That faculty is what has made Northern Dancer and his offspring, too, go a lot farther than people thought they should, because everybody thought he was basically a miler or something like that. But he had this ability to accelerate and you could rate him, and that's the same way with many of his sons."

At Keeneland, the bidding usually came down to duels between the British syndicates headed by Robert Sangster, the soccer pools baron, and the various Arab interests led by Sheikh Mohammed Bin Rashid al Maktoum of the United Arab Emirates nation of Dubai.

As a spellbound breeding industry held its breath, the prices spiraled to dizzying heights early in the 1980s. Sangster broke the world record in 1981 by paying $3.5 million for a son of Northern Dancer, then broke it a year later with a $4.25 million bid for a son of Nijinsky II. In 1983, determined to not be outbid, Sheikh Mohammed's Aston Upthorpe Stud went all the way to $10.2 million for a Northern Dancer colt out of the mare My Bupers. That record lasted only two years, or until Sangster topped the 1985 sale by spending $13.1 million for a son of Nijinsky II out of the mare My Charmer, the dam of 1977 Triple Crown winner Seattle Slew. The consignor was breeder Warner Jones Jr. of the Hermitage Farm of Goshen, Kentucky.

Not a bad record for a little horse who once could have been bought for $25,000 and barely escaped being gelded. But Northern Dancer had as much heart and courage as any horse who has ever set foot on the American turf. Or, as Jim Murray of the *Los Angeles Times* wrote after his 1964 Derby win, "He's so plucky there's barely room in him for his heart. His legs are barely long enough to keep his tail off the ground. He probably takes a hundred more strides than anybody in a race, but he's harder to pass up than a third martini."

GRAUSTARK AND PROUD CLARION
A Bittersweet Twist of Fate

[Keeneland program, April 2002]

This is the story about the vagaries of Kentucky Derby luck. It involves a hallowed old Bluegrass breeding farm, emotional tugs on a great owner's heart, an undistinguished trainer nicknamed "Boo," and an odd couple of thoroughbred colts.

The Blue Grass Stakes at Keeneland, now the Toyota Blue Grass, provided the stage for crucial scenes in the melodrama. When it was over, an old dinner bell rang out a haunting reminder of the luck, romance, mystery, tradition, unpredictability, joy, and heartbreak that make horse racing special.

In the spring of 1966, a colt named Graustark arrived at Keeneland accompanied by so much hype that his trainer, Loyd "Boo" Gentry, was a nervous, fidgety, impatient wreck. The colt was owned by Darby Dan Farm, which was located on what used to be Col. E.R. Bradley's Idle Hour Stock Farm on Old Frankfort Pike near Keeneland.

When John Galbreath, the Columbus, Ohio, industrialist and philanthropist, bought the farm, he named it in honor of a road on his farm in Ohio (Darby Creek Road) and his son (Dan). By the time Graustark came around, the farm already had won the Kentucky Derby with Chateaugay in 1963. In addition, Galbreath owned the Pittsburgh Pirates baseball team, which had won the World Series in 1960. (In 1972, Galbreath won the Epsom Derby with a colt named after his favorite Pirate, Roberto Clemente).

The farm was managed by Olin Gentry, who was involved with four

Trainer Loyd "Boo" Gentry.

Derby winners while working for Col. Bradley in the 1920s and '30s. He didn't get along well with Jimmy Conway, who trained Chateaugay, and Conway abruptly resigned in Graustark's 2-year-old year. Gentry, with Galbreath's blessing, then turned the Darby Dan job over to his nephew, Loyd, who had never trained a great horse nor won a classic race.

A son of Ribot, Graustark was the kind of horse that make horsemen dream. He won both his starts as a 2-year-old, and his first four at 3, easily outclassing his opposition. Racing experts were calling him a "superhorse" and "the best 3-year-old since Citation." Joe Hirsch, the esteemed columnist for *The Daily Racing Form*, had his stride measured during a workout and found that it compared favorably with the immortal Man o' War.

"Did you ever see DiMaggio play baseball?" Hirsch asked on a chilly morning at Keeneland. "Well, Graustark is like DiMaggio. He makes it look easy. The action makes the horse, you know, and his action is magnificent."

On the day of the Blue Grass, Loyd Gentry admitted that another Graustark victory would guarantee a small Derby field at Churchill Downs. "But if we lose," Gentry said, "they won't have room for the people over there. A lot of things can happen in the next 10 days (then the time between the Blue Grass and the Derby)."

The race was held over a sloppy track on a cold, rainy afternoon at Keeneland. Faced with only two opponents, Graustark carried jockey Braulio Baeza to a 10-length lead on the backstretch and seemed destined to win by as much as Baeza wanted.

But then, suddenly, Graustark began to slow down and a little colt named Abe's Hope began to make up ground on him. "Dad and I were together in a box that day," recalled Dan Galbreath years later, "Right away I said, 'Something's wrong . . . This can't be.'"

At the head of the stretch, Abe's Hope took the lead, but Graustark dug in and was beaten by only a nose at the wire, It turned out that he had run more than a mile on a fractured cannon bone in his left foreleg. His only defeat also was his most courageous performance.

"I ran down to talk to Baeza as soon as he got off," said Dan Galbreath. "Baeza showed me his hand, where he had held tight to the rein to keep Graustark from bearing out. He couldn't open it, and it was white because he had gripped so hard. Dad didn't say anything. He went home."

After Kauai King won the Derby, *Sports Illustrated* ran a story entitled "Boo Made a Boo-Boo." It accused the trainer of working Graustark so hard that it led to a heel injury in Florida and lameness after an easy win at Keeneland. The article, written by Pete Axthelm, also accused Olin Gentry of running off Conway so his nephew could train Graustark.

"I had nothing to do with his (Conway's) quitting and couldn't care less," Olin Gentry retorted. "But I will say this: Loyd trained him a damned sight better than Conway or anybody else could have. Loyd did a good job. It was just an unfortunate accident for the horse."

For the next 12 months, Loyd Gentry brooded over the criticism. He wasn't much distracted by Proud Clarion, a son of Hail to Reason who seemed to be more or less a plodder. If Graustark was DiMaggio, Proud Clarion was Eddie Gaedel, the midget that Bill Veeck once used to pinch-hit for the St. Louis Browns. Even when Proud Clarion finished second to Diplomat Way in the Blue Grass nobody seemed impressed.

After the Blue Grass, jockey Baeza declined to renew his contract with Darby Dan, so Olin and Loyd picked Bobby Ussery to ride Proud Clarion in Louisville. On the Tuesday before the Derby, Loyd talked about Graustark on the way to watch Proud Clarion put in his final serious work.

I don't worry about that now," he said. "At the time, that was one of my biggest disappointments. It was a shock, even though it didn't happen suddenly. I had been suspicioning for a day or two that something was wrong with Graustark. But once things happen, well, that's that. I can get in the car now and not even think about Graustark." Proud Clarion worked a mile and an eighth in 1:58 on a muddy track. "Very slow, but that's all right," Gentry said. Later he amended that to say, "I'm not real hot

Proud Clarion and jockey Braulio Baeza.

39

Owner John Galbreath (far right) with baseball great Pete Rose, Rose's friend Bill Sena, and Olin Gentry (far left).

on my horse's workout. In fact, it was terrible."

The Derby crowd wasn't very hot on Proud Clarion, dismissing him at odds of 30-1 in the 14-horse field. But Ussery saved ground on the inside in the early going, eased him out after the half-mile pole, and took dead aim on the pacesetting Barbs Delight.

Second at the top of the stretch, Proud Clarion passed Barbs Delight at the eighth pole and hung on for a length victory that paid his backers $62.20 for a $2 win bet.

Loyd Gentry was jubilant despite a case of hepatitis and yellow jaundice. "Everybody expected Graustark to win, but nobody expected this horse to win," Gentry said in a soggy winner's circle. "I would have to say that it's even a bigger thrill to win with a 30-1 shot than a horse that would have gone off at, say, 2-1. I've waited 42 years for this, but I've especially waited the last 12 months."

But for John Galbreath, even Proud Clarion's Derby win didn't make up for Graustark's breakdown. "I'd say it was his biggest disappointment," his son said years later.

That was at least partly because Galbreath was shrewd enough to know that Proud Clarion's win was more fluke than certification of greatness. Indeed, the colt was retired after his 4-year-old season with only six wins to show for 25 starts and a modest $218,730 in career earnings.

A few minutes after Proud Clarion's win, groom William Sanders, who watched the race on TV at Darby Dan, began ringing the farm's own proud clarion, sending peals of victory through the gloom of a cloudy day and across the undulating Bluegrass countryside. Decades earlier, while working for Col. Bradley, Sanders had rung the bell to celebrate the Derby wins of Bubbling Over (1926), Burgoo King (1932), and Brokers Tip (1933). He also rang it for Chateaugay.

"I rang the old bell to keep everything in order," Sanders said. "If Graustark had run last year, we would have rung it two years in a row. But I wasn't surprised by Proud Clarion. He ran such a good race in the Blue Grass at Keeneland that I thought he could win the Derby."

CANONERO II
"Viva Venezuela!"

[*Sports Illustrated*, May 1971]

By now everyone should be aware that something strange and wonderful is happening in thoroughbred racing. It all revolves around a big colt of copper hue named Canonero II, who was bred in Kentucky, developed in Venezuela and now seems destined for Valhalla. He already has won the Kentucky Derby and the Preakness, making him the darling of the American turf and the biggest hero in Venezuela since Simon Bolivar. Now he needs only the Belmont Stakes on June 5 at New York's Belmont Park to capture that symbol of superiority known as the Triple Crown.

Seldom has a horse story so enchanted the American public. This is the colt who was first sold for $1,200 and is now worth $5 million—perhaps even more if he wins the Belmont. This is the colt who is owned, trained and ridden by an unlikely trio of Venezuelans who cannot speak English but can put on quite some fiesta when led to a winner's circle. And this is the colt who will have all the underdog lovers in the land yelling "Vive!" when he attempts to finish his job on the Establishment in the Belmont.

Nobody better understands the phenomenon of Canonero than Juan Arias, the colt's bright young trainer. "He is a horse of destiny," says Arias, a romantic in ways other than the use of language. "He is the champion of all the people—black and white, rich and poor, American and Venezuelan, everyone." That Canonero will take the Triple Crown last won by Citation in 1948 now seems logical enough. As Arias puts it, "We only have to worry about a horse we haven't seen. If we run against the same horses we beat in the first two races,

Billy Reed with Pedro Baptista and Canonero II.

Canonero will win even more easily." That being the case, some of the stuffier members of the racing establishment may be relieved to know that if Canonero wins the Crown, it will not become the possession of just any old Tom, Dick and Juan. The people behind Canonero are sound, experienced horsemen by anybody's standards.

"I have a right to be taken seriously, and so do my horse and my jockey and my people," says Arias, whose pride and dignity were offended by the belittling attitude of much of the press and many racing professionals even after the Derby. "They say we are clowns. They say we are Indians because my horse gallops slowly, sometimes without a saddle. They come to look at my horse but turn away and wrinkle up their noses. But now I no longer have to justify myself. What can they say now?"

The colt now known as Canonero II was bred in Kentucky by Edward Benjamin. His sire, Pretendre, was beaten by a nose by Charlttown in the 1966 Epson Derby, and his dam, Dixieland II, was a stakes winner at 3. Not bad breeding—but still, Luis Neves, a Venezuelan agent, was able to pick him up for only $1,200 at the 1969 Keeneland Fall Sales. Neves shipped the colt straight to Venezuela, where he quickly sold him to Pedro Baptista for 26,000 bolivars, which is about $6,500.

Baptista, 44, is the owner of Crown T (Chrome Everything), a factory in Caracas that produces a wide assortment of chrome products and furniture including beds for the Navy. The business, started by Baptista's grandfather in 1901, was running at about $25,000 a year when Pedro went to work there in 1942. Now it does $1.5 million annually, and is the largest of its kind in

Venezuela. "I used to work 18 hours a day," says Baptista. "Now I only work 8 or 10."

Baptista is married and has three children, a son and two married daughters. (The son, Pedro Jr., 17, accepted the Derby trophy in his father's absence). One of the wealthiest men in Caracas, Baptista lives in a castle, or "castilo," once owned by the dictator Marcos Perez Jimenez, who was deposed in 1958. He has his own private discotheque in the basement.

A stumpy, swarthy man with a scar on his nose and few teeth, Baptista is considered something of an eccentric at home. "You will see him in downtown Caracas and he looks like a bum," says a friend. "No tie, no teeth, unshaven, baggy suit. But he probably has thousands of dollars in his pocket." After the races at La Rinconada in Caracas, Baptista and Arias sometimes relax at the castillo, and Arias always is amused to see Don Pedro padding around in his favorite pair of sneakers. He does not drink, but smokes 80 cigarettes a day.

Baptista has owned horses since 1950, and at its peak his stable included more than 50 head. Now he races only about six. His introduction to the vagaries of ownership was hardly encouraging. "I bought nine horses," he says, "and none was a winner. That made me superstitious, so now I never race a horse in my own name." In Caracas, he uses two hybrid names for his stable—Vigleyepe and Glalu, both made up from combinations of the first letters in his family's surnames. In the U.S., he has raced Canonero in the name of his son-in-law, Edgar Caibett, but Caibett not only owns no part of Canonero, he has never seen him run; "I am the sole owner," says Baptista. "I do not race the horse in my name because I am superstitious."

After buying the colt from Neves, the first thing Baptista did was name him Canonero II. A canonero is a group of people singing, accompanied by a small four-string guitar, a gourd and a regular guitar. At the Plaza de Bolivar in Caracas, the corner where the musicians gather is called "el rincon canonero" and this is where Baptista got the name. The "II" is there because there was an earlier Canonero.

When Baptista first turned over Canonero to Arias, the colt looked as if he would be lucky to develop into a decent claimer, much less a Triple Crown candidate. He was small, he had a split right rear hoof, and he had worms. After treatment the hoof took three months to heal, but the worms were a more difficult problem. "We had to clean out his stomach every 30 days," recalls Baptista, "and I had to get him special food, like seaweed from Australia."

Though Canonero grew to be a strong colt, Baptista still didn't think he was much of a horse. He was so unimpressed, in fact, that when the colt finally went to the races, the jockey Baptista hired was E. Cointreras, a hapless rider who had not won a race in 15 years. "He was so bad," says a friend of Baptista, "that the other jockeys called him 'Willie Shoemaker' to make fun of him."

One can only imagine what Cointreras said to the other jockeys after Canonero breezed home by six lengths in his first race, a six-furlong handicap on August 8, 1970, in La Rinconada.

Nobody was more pleased than Arias. Born on a farm in Venezuela's central plains area, Arias, now 32, grew up in poverty. His father died when Juan was four and two years later he and his mother moved to Caracas. When his mother gave him money to go to the movies or an amusement park, Arias would sneak off to the race track, to visit the horses and sweep out the stalls for free. Later, when a hernia prevented him from becoming a pilot in the Air Force, he turned to horses and racing. From 1955 through 1959 he was a student in the government's school for horse trainers. "The idea was to produce some Venezuelan professionals," says Arias. "At the time the top trainers in the country were from England, Mexico, Peru and other countries." Arias received his training license on July 4, 1959 and embarked on a career that, for eight years, was dogged by failure and defeat.

"The only horses that I had I got by force, and they were *perros* (dogs)," he says. "It was terrible. I slept in the barns and I didn't know where my next meal was coming from. Most of my classmates quit training and they advised me to quit, too. I guess the only reason I kept going was because I was young and single.

"I remember once a fellow around the track came up to me and said, 'You're not good for anything, hombre, where did you get your diploma from? Out of a box of talcum powder?' I looked at him and I said, 'First of all, I don't depend on you for food. Second, it doesn't make any difference where I got my diploma from. And third, someday I will prove that I am a better trainer than anybody.'"

Arias' fortunes began to change in 1967, when a mutual friend introduced him to Baptista. At the time, Baptista's stable was in a slump. He put 16 horses in Arias' hands and promised him a three-month trial. The stable won 700,000 bolivars during that time, and soon Arias was training the entire string. His biggest achievement before the Derby came in the 1968 Pella de Potrancas (Pot of the Fillies) when his horses ran 1-2-3 and won a total of $117,500. "That was my biggest thrill in racing," says Baptista, "and you should have seen Arias. He was so loco that I had to get a doctor for him."

A short man with gray flecks in his black hair and smooth skin the color of cocoa, Arias is by far the liveliest, most visible member of Canonero's party. When he is not working with horses, he likes to drink Scotch, dance the Joropo and swim in the ocean. He plans to marry a girl in Colombia as soon as he wins a divorce from his present wife. But these entanglements have not prevented him from doing a little playful flirting while in the U.S.

"It is a natural tendency for us to throw flowers to women," he says. "It is the oldest race in the world—women after men, and men after women. I am jealous about my women and I am jealous about my horses—nothing else. I find that you must treat horses like women, speaking softly to them and knowing when to give them love pats.

"When I find that I am flirting with a married woman, I apologize to her husband and tell him something like 'May God take care of her and conserve her for you.' And if I find myself with an older lady, I tell her she has the sparkle in her eye of a 15-year-old."

Arias is more secretive about his training methods, but often hints that his ways are different, and special, and that someday he will write a book about them. "I can learn from the American trainers," he says, "but I can also teach them some things."

One tactic Arias admits to is talking to Canonero before a race to psyche him up. "Juan believes that his horses can understand him and help him discover what to do," says a Venezuelan friend. "Do you remember the day before the Preakness, when Juan paraded Canonero in the winner's circle? Many said it was to familiarize him with the crowd and the track. That is baloney. He was trying to use psychology on him, to show him where he wanted him to go."

After Canonero's first win as a 2-year-old, Baptista and Arias shipped him to Del Mar in California, where he was third and fifth in two starts. "We thought that an American horse should race in America," said Juan. "Mr. Baptista told me on the plane to California that if Canonero won, or if he ran well, he wanted to point him for the Kentucky Derby."

Gustavo Avila, the bushy-browed, taciturn jockey who rode Canonero in the Derby and Preakness, joined the team on March 7 of this year, when he guided the colt to a 2-1/2-length victory in a mile-and-a-quarter race at La Rinconada. The time was slow—2:08—but it demonstrated the stamina that has stood the colt in good stead in his two Triple Crown races.

Avila, 31, is considered the premier jockey in Venezuela, or, as Arias puts it, "He is the ace of spades, the ace of jockeys, the ace of men." He did not get on a horse until he was 13 when, on the advice of some school friends, he entered a school for jockeys. "I was terrible," Avila says now, breaking into a rare grin. "In fact, they kicked me out of school several times because I kept falling off."

In Venezuela, Avila is known as "El Monstruo"—the Monster—a nickname of respect among the chalk players who have watched him boot home many long-shots. Over his 17-year career Avila has won more than 1,250 races, including five victories in the most important race in Venezuela—the Clasico de Simon de Bolivar. Avila is proud of his 1962 record: he won more times (95) than he finished out of the money (78). If his achievements seem modest by American and European standards, it should be noted that racing in Venezuela is held only on Saturdays and Sundays. Avila estimates his annual earnings at between $50,000 and $60,000, and he and Arias enjoy teasing each other about their alleged bolivar-pinching.

One night shortly after the Preakness, the teasing began while they were sitting in a bar drinking Scotch.

Arias: "I'm going to change my money into $5 bills and fill a room full. Like Scrooge McDuck, I will need a shovel."

Avila: "Bah, Arias is too tight. He hasn't even bought me a Coca-Cola to toast Canonero."

Arias: "Avila's hobby is collecting bolivars. He has about five or six trunks full. Every day he drags them out into his yard and he takes the money out to sun. He has bulldogs and German Shepherds walking around him in circles for protection. Then he gets his rakes and shovels and puts the money back in the trunks. And besides, Avila, I don't toast anybody with Coca-Cola."

After his initial victory with Canonero, Avila rode the colt twice more, finishing third and first. But then he was replaced by R.Z. Guzman. The theory, according to Arias, was that Avila was too busy to give Canonero more than perfunctory attention. Guzman won his first race aboard Canonero, but on April 10, in the colt's last race before the Derby, Guzman and Canonero were third by 3-3/4 lengths in a 1-1/8-mile handicap—and Baptista began to have misgivings about sending him to Louisville. "We couldn't figure it out," says Arias. "He ran good and he was in good shape. We finally decided it must have been the jockey's fault."

Soon Baptista was on the phone to Avila.

"Gustavo, you are rich and famous now," he remembers saying, "but do you want to be more rich and famous? If so, I will let you ride Canonero in the Derby."

Venezuelan racing fans generally thought Baptista was loco to even dream about winning the Derby. "They said Canonero would finish last at Churchill Downs," he recalls. "They said Avila would lose by 10 lengths. They said I was throwing my money away. But I knew what I was doing and that everybody else was crazy."

Nevertheless, Baptista did not make the trip to Louisville, because of pressing business commitments. The colt was kept in Caracas until only a few days before the Derby because, says Baptista, "I wanted to keep him where I could see him as long as possible." The plane carrying Canonero had trouble and returned to Caracas, but that apparently didn't bother the colt as much as his traveling companions—chickens and ducks. "He didn't like the other animals," says Baptista, "so we sent him to Louisville by truck."

Immediately after the Derby, one of Baptista's friends in Miami called the owner to tell him the news. "That's a sick joke," said Baptista, angrily slamming down the receiver. Seconds later the friend called back to tell him it was the truth. Baptista began to cry and could not talk. While Baptista was crying, his 74-year-old father came in and asked, "What's happening?" Told the news, he too began to cry. Then father and son went outside, got in a car and drove to the grave of Baptista's mother, where they cried some more. "They wished that she could be with them," said Luiz Efren Ruiz, a close friend of Baptista. "Then Don Pedro promised the Virgin Mary that he would build a grotto for his garden with a golden Virgin inside. That is already done."

At the Preakness, Baptista showed up with a lively party of 10 friends, and he remained in Baltimore until the Thursday after the race. During that time, he could usually be found in the hotel coffee shop, chain-smoking and mulling over Canonero's future. On Monday, he said, a syndicate of U.S. horsemen offered $5,000,000 for the colt. On Wednesday, the president of Venezuela called to say that his government would match the offer. "There would be a revolution," said Victor Shalon, who is Baptista's accountant and friend. "What we need in Venezuela are houses, not horses."

No matter. Baptista was enjoying the notoriety. "It is amazing to me," he said, "that a black man (Arias) and two Indians (Baptista and Avila) could come here and smash 200 years of tradition in racing. And now, God willing, Canonero also will win the Belmont and then what a fiesta we will have in Venezuela!"

That should be something to see, judging by what has already happened. When Avila returned to Caracas on the weekend between the Derby and the Preakness, he was carried through the streets. He also managed to win three races, including one aboard Pretendido, a half-brother to Canonero. On Preakness afternoon, racing was suspended at La Rinconada so the fans could watch Canonero on 100 TV sets set up for the occasion. When Canonero crossed the finish line, the fans were so delirious that they broke all the TV screens.

There is much reflected glory from Canoneros' achievements, but the man whose life would seem to be changed the most is Arias. Before the Derby, he was so little known that a Caracas newspaper could only find some old picture of him in its files—and even that took some hunting. "Now even his fellow trainers will be waiting to cut off his tie and parade him through the streets," says a friend.

"Ah, yes, it is nice to think about," said Arias one afternoon recently. Then he laughed. "You know, in my country, my friends know me as 'Juan Bimba.'" That means a man of the people, not an aristocrat. When I go back, I will still be 'Juan Bimba.' I will still be a man of the people."

[Epilogue: Bothered by illness and injury, Canonero II finished fourth in the 1971 Belmont, won by Pass Catcher. A record crowd of 81,000, including many Hispanics, showed up at Belmont Park to cheer him.]

SECRETARIAT
"A Tremedous Machine"

[From the *Lexington Herald-Leader,* October 1989]

Here came the big red horse, turning for home at New York's Belmont Park, the sun glinting off his copper coat as he drew away, opening an incredible lead while the crowd, standing, shrieked an animal shriek that grew until it was thunder, shaking the grandstand to its foundation.

The date was June 9, 1973, and Secretariat was giving racing not only its first Triple Crown winner in a quarter of a century, but a virtuoso performance that took the breath away, literally, and caused even the most jaded of eyes to grow misty.

As he pounded down the stretch, so alone and so exquisite in his splendor, announcer Chic Anderson made the call for the CBS television network: "Secretariat by 12, Secretariat by 14, Secretariat is moving like a tremendous machine!"

Nearing the wire, jockey Ron Turcotte sneaked a peak at the times blinking on the infield tote board. He was shocked because not even he expected a win like this. The final margin, 31 lengths, and the time, 2:24 for the mile and a half, are records that stand to this day.

It was perfect, and beautiful, and remarkable. And it's what a man remembers most now, in the wake of the news that Secretariat has been humanely destroyed at Claiborne Farm because of a hoof disease that couldn't be healed. He was in his 19th year and he is mourned by millions, especially those dear hearts and gentle people who, to his dying day, were sending him bits of candy, or fan letters asking, pretty please, for one of his shoes or a strand of his mane.

He was a hero in his heyday, such blessed relief from the depressing news of Vietnam and Watergate that even *Time* and *Newsweek* put him on its covers, and he has remained a hero through the years—a symbol of excellence and majesty that could never be tarnished and needed no burnishing.

Today there are some, even in this state where horse racing is a way of life, who will say it is rather silly to get all weepy over the death of a horse, no matter how good he may have been.

To those cold hearts and callous souls, we should give our sympathy, for they will never feel nor understand the soaring, transcendent joy that, in all of sport, can only be inspired by the sight of a great thoroughbred, running free. Think of the sheer athleticism of the young Muhammad Ali, the grace of Joe DiMaggio in his prime, the bullishness of Larry Csonka, the elegance of Julius Erving. All that, and more, belonged to Secretariat, who still is what every breeder has in mind every time he sends a mare to be mated to a stallion.

Remembering Secretariat, a man went to the archives to find what the late Joe Palmer wrote years ago about another immortal chestnut, Man o' War. It went, in part, like this: "He was as near to a living flame as horses ever get, and horses get closer to this than anything else. It was not merely that he smashed his opposition, sometimes by a hundred lengths, or that he set world records, or that he cared not a tinker's curse for weight or distance or track or horses.

"It was even that when he was standing motionless in his stall, with his ears pricked forward and his eyes focused on something slightly above the horizon which mere people never see, energy still poured from him. He could get in no position which suggested actual repose, and his very stillness was that of the coiled spring, of the crouched tiger . . ."

Palmer felt there had never been a horse like Man o' War, nor could ever be again. You have to wonder if he would have changed his mind, had he only lived long enough to see Secretariat, especially during the Triple Crown campaign in the spring of 1973.

Upset by stablemate Angle Light in the Wood Memorial, his last race before the Kentucky Derby, Secretariat had a lot of people wondering when he came to Churchill Downs.

The most nervous weren't his old-money owner, Mrs. Penny Tweedy of Virginia's Meadow Stable, nor his stumpy little Canadian-born trainer, Lucien Laurin, but the breeders who already had put up $6.08 million, then a world record, for exclusive lifetime breeding rights to him.

All Secretariat did, of course, was run the greatest Triple Crown series ever. Before his *piece de resistance* in the Belmont, he covered the Derby's mile and a quarter in 1:59-2/5, still the record, and the Preakness's mile and three-sixteenths in 1:53-2/5, another record that later was unfairly amended to 1:54-

Billy Reed and his daughter Susan visit the great Secretariat at Claiborne Farm.

2/5 because of a malfunction in the official timer.

In the Preakness, he made a move in the first turn, moving from back in the pack to the lead, that will be recalled until Baltimore runs out of crab cakes.

Later in the year, running against older horses, he was upset by Onion, in Saratoga's Whitney, and Prove Out, in Belmont's Woodward, and his detractors, old-timers mostly, would use those races to argue that he wasn't as good as the likes of Man o' War and Citation.

Maybe they were right, and maybe not, but they were definitely missing the point. Secretariat was to his generation of fans what Man o' War and Citation were to theirs. And as the first Triple Crown winner of the television age, he did more good for racing's image than any horse ever.

He was retired and taken to Claiborne, at the end of his 3-year-old season. When he arrived at the farm, long the home of many of the world's best sires, he was given the same stall in the stallion barn that had been occupied by his sire, the great Bold Ruler.

On that bittersweet afternoon, after all the photographers and curiosity-seekers had left, Secretariat was left alone with his groom, Eddie Sweat, and a reporter.

Looking into Secretariat's stall, Sweat made a chirping sound, which caused the big red horse to prick his ears and move closer to the door.

"Well, it's all over now," Sweat crooned, ever so softly. "They'll never forget you, big fella. Never."

They never did, and they never will. The flame has been extinguished, but the memory will glow so long as there are people who will always wonder if they'll ever again see another quite as good as Secretariat, the big red horse who stole the country's heart.

SEATTLE SLEW
The People's Horse

[The Churchill Downs Website, May 2002]

The "People's Horse" died in his sleep on Tuesday, May 7, 2002, precisely a quarter of century from the day he won the 103rd Kentucky Derby at Churchill Downs. He drew his last breath at the Hill n' Dale Farm just outside Lexington, Kentucky, where he was quietly trying to recover from throat surgery to relieve spinal-cord compression due to arthritic changes in his vertebrae.

As potent in the breeding shed as he was on the track, Slew was bred for the final time on February 23. The mare's name was Dimontina. His owners, Mickey and Karen Taylor, had hoped he would be able to resume his breeding career at Three Chimneys Farm late this spring. So had Slew, who, at age 28, would get so excited when mares were unloaded at the receiving barn that Tom Wade, his longtime companion, had to turn the radio to full volume so Slew couldn't hear the mares whinny.

But now he's gone to wherever Triple Crown winners go when they die. Of the 11 colts who have swept the Kentucky Derby, Preakness Stakes and Belmont Stakes, Slew is the only one to do it while still unbeaten. He might have retired unbeaten had the Taylors and their partners, Dr. Jim and Sally Hill, let trainer Billy Turner continue to call the shots.

However, instead of honoring Turner's desire to give Slew a long break after the Belmont, the owners ordered him to ship Slew to California to pick up what appeared to be easy money in the Swaps Stakes. Alas for his many fans, the weary Slew finished a dull fourth to J.O. Tobin. It proved to be his worst finish in a 17-race career that included 14 victories and two seconds.

A son of Bold Reasoning out of My Charmer, Slew was bred in Kentucky by Ben Castleman. He was the "People's Horse" because he was purchased at the 1975 Fasig-Tipton of Kentucky yearling sale for only $17,500 due to perceived flaws in his pedigree and conformation. (The highest price for a Derby winner was the $4 million paid for Fusaichi Pegasus in 1998.)

He was the poor kid from the other side of the tracks thumbing his nose at the bluebloods, and the public ate it up. In the movie business, Secretariat would have been Robert Redford and Slew would have been Al Pacino. But everyone rooted for him because he was the poster boy for the idea that you didn't have to be a multi-millionaire to own a terrific horse.

In addition, Slew was surrounded by a bunch of charming young people who were fresh to the game and overwhelmed by their good luck. Mickey Taylor was a lumberman from White Swan, Washington, his wife a former airline attendant. Dr. Hill was a racetrack veterinarian in Florida, Turner an unknown former steeplechase rider, and jockey Jean Cruguet a journeyman who had never won a Triple Crown race.

Slew almost lost the Derby when he stumbled virtually to his knees coming out of the starting gate, but Cruguet steadied him, then bulled his way between horses to get his accustomed spot at the front of the pack. Turning for home, Slew seized the lead from For the Moment, then easily held off Run Dusty Run's late bid for a 1-1/2-length victory.

"It was Slew's greatest performance," Turner said years later. "He got left at the gate, he got blocked, he got shut off. But he ran like a wild horse. He ran over horses. Man o' War couldn't have done it. It will go down as one of the greatest horse races ever."

After the unique rigors and raucous surroundings of the Derby, the Preakness was a stroll in the park for Slew, who held off Iron Constitution by a workmanlike 1-1/2-lengths. But when he headed for the Belmont and his rendezvous with destiny, there were still doubters such as W.E. "Smiley" Adams, the trainer of Run Dusty Run, and Thomas F. Root Jr., trainer of Iron Constitution.

Remembering how the Derby crowd had excited Slew, Turner kept him in the barn until the last minute. His plan was to be the last to arrive at the paddock, saddle Slew quickly, and get him out on the track before he got too worked up by the photographers and the fans. Although he was subsequently fined $200 for being late to the paddock, Turner figured that was a small price to pay for a slice of immortality.

After the field left the paddock, Turner ducked into a grandstand bar to watch the race on TV. He asked the bartender for a vodka-tonic, but was told to get to the back of the line. So a reporter friend (blush) got the drink for him, then called the race for him because Turner's vision was blocked by leaping, screaming fans.

As soon as he saw Slew's black-and-gold silks flash past in front, Turner ran out of the bar, jumped a fence to the tunnel leading to the track, and had to convince a Pinkerton guard that he was, indeed, the trainer of the Triple Crown winner. Then, for the first time all year, he got in the winner's circle photo.

The next day, Turner showed up at his barn in a black 1932 Franklin, a luxury car from the Bonnie-and-Clyde era equipped with running boards, oversized head lamps, and white sidewall tires.

"When you win a horse race," Turner said, "a racetracker always gets a big, new car. I'm just trying this one out. What do you think?"

"Well," said Mick Kennedy, Slew's exercise boy, "I bet it doesn't run as smooth as Slew."

After doing his interviews, Turner retired to his "office," which is what he called Esposito's Tavern, located across the street from Belmont's back stable gate. The Esposito brothers, John and Junior, already had painted the jockey standing on the bar's front yard with Slew's colors.

The fiasco in California turned out to be Turner's last race as Slew's trainer. It had knocked the nearly-black colt out of the Travers Stakes at Saratoga, a point that Turner made so often and so loudly that the owners finally canned him in favor of Doug Peterson, who was perfectly willing to be a "yes-man" trainer.

Under Peterson, Slew didn't return to the track until 1978, He made seven starts as a 4-year-old, winning five and finishing second twice. The owners fired Cruguet after a nose loss to Dr. Patches at Monmouth and replaced him with Angel Cordero, Jr. for his last four races, one of which was a three-length win over 1978 Triple Crown winner Affirmed in the Marlboro Cup.

His final loss came to Exceller in the 1 1/2-mile Jockey Club Gold Cup on October 14, 1978, and it also may have been one of Slew's greatest performances. On a "sloppy" track, he led throughout the early going, was overtaken by Exceller at the top of the stretch, then fought back to lose by only a nose. It was a classic example of his speed, strength, stamina, and will to win. "I think that race is the one that really sold the breeders on him," Taylor said.

Initially, Slew was sent to Spendthrift Farm because Brownell Combs had paid $6 million for half of him. It was here that he hooked up with Tom Wade, who followed him to Three Chimneys when Spendthrift began having financial problems.

As a sire, the "People's Horse" produced a lot of racing aristocrats. His offspring include more than 100 stakes winners, including champions A. P. Indy, Swale, Slew o' Gold, Landaluce, Capote, and Surfside. He also is the broodmare sire of Cigar, a two-time Horse of the Year, and appears in the

Billy Reed with Seattle Slew.

broodmare pedigrees of Tiznow, Kona Gold, and Golden Ballet.

All told, his offspring earned more than $75 million.

The other Triple Crown winners, for the most part, were owned by pillars of the racing establishment, so their lives didn't change much. But Slew's tour de force definitely changed the lives of his connections, especially the Taylors. When Slew underwent his first surgery in 2000, they moved from Washington to be near him.

And after his second surgery, they parked a silver Airstream trailer next to his barn that served as a sort of mobile office. They moved him from Three Chimneys to Hill n' Dale only a few weeks ago to provide Slew more privacy and serenity as he coped with his recovery and with the aging process.

Every year, the "People's Horse" received a slew of notes, cards, and flowers from fans who remembered seeing him run. He was truly great, easily one of the eight or ten best horses ever produced in America.

The sadness over his death is more than counterbalanced by the richness of his legacy. As Mickey Taylor recently put it, "He was the real McCoy, the best of the best. He's done it all, at every level."

ALYDAR AND CALUMET
Our Old Kentucky Home

[From the *Lexington Herald-Leader*, March 1992]

From the equine cemetery at the back of the farm, where the legends are buried beneath weather-beaten granite headstones, you could see the huge auction tent, striped red and white, that had been erected there in the midst of Calumet Farm, just up the road from the old white mansion.

This was the day that was never supposed to come, the moment that never could be imagined by anybody who ever saw, or even heard tell of, the mighty thoroughbreds who had campaigned in the devil's red and blue, the most feared and famous silks the sport had ever known.

To stroll through the cemetery is to invite goosebumps.

Even if you've never particularly been a racing fan, surely you've heard of Whirlaway and Citation, of trainer Plain Ben Jones and his son Jimmy, of the record eight Kentucky Derby wins, of jockey Eddie Arcaro and all the great ones, ghosts now, that he booted home in the 1940s and '50s, the glory years for Calumet.

But yesterday, on an appropriately gray and blustery morning in the Bluegrass, the unthinkable was to transpire. Proud Calumet, finally brought low by years of incredible mismanagement that led to $127 million in debts, was to be auctioned off, just as if it were a common cattle farm.

In the moments before the opening gavel dropped at 11 a.m., the mood inside the tent was funereal. Some of the 5,000 or so who occupied the white folding chairs had come to bid on something—the four parcels of farm property, the Calumet name, the 1939 horse van that carried the legends, a Calumet blanket, whatever.

But most had come to simply pay their respects. To understand, you have to know the special feelings of esteem that Kentuckians, even those not directly involved in the racing industry, have held for Calumet for more than five decades.

Because it has been such a shining symbol of excellence and success in a state where poverty and ignorance have long been chronic problems, Calumet—not Federal Hill in Bardstown—has really been, in many minds, the Old Kentucky Home of Stephen Foster's melancholy song, the one sung every year as the horses come on the track for the Kentucky Derby.

Weep no more, my lady
Oh! weep no more today
We will sing one song
For my old Kentucky home
For my old Kentucky home, far away

But yesterday those who came to weep were in for an extraordinarily pleasant surprise. After 11 tense minutes of bidding, the main tract of land—including the main house, the training tracks, the veterinary clinic, all of the important stuff—was sold to a respected horseman who immediately vowed, to wild huzzahs all around, that he would maintain Calumet and "not change a single blade of grass."

As if he needed to back up his $17 million purchase of the main tract with an exclamation point, buyer Henryk deKwiatkowski then paid $210,000 for the Calumet name. When the auctioneer screamed, "The man who bought the farm has also bought the name," another roar of relief and happiness went up from the audience.

Somewhere up in horsey heaven, Admiral Gene Markey had to be chuckling with approval and pleasure. He was the second husband of Lucille Wright Markey, whose first husband, Warren Wright, built the Calumet equine empire on the fortune he had inherited from his father, the founder of the Calumet Baking Powder Company.

Unlike Wright, who took a stern, no-nonsense approach to business, the Admiral was a bon vivant whose many pursuits included writing screenplays for motion pictures. Alas, he wasn't nearly as successful at writing as he was at marrying gorgeous actresses. His three wives prior to Mrs. Markey were Joan Bennett, Hedy Lamarr and Myrna Loy.

But what happened yesterday at Calumet sounded like something out of one of the Admiral's corny scripts. Just when the debtors were getting ready to foreclose on the old homestead, here came a dashing hero—deKwiatkowski, an airplane-manufacturing magnate who claims to have been a Polish flying ace in World War II—to save the day.

The word "claims" appears in the previous paragraph because when deKwiatkowski first told his war stories after winning the 1982 Belmont Stakes with Conquistador Cielo, the ever-vigilant media soon discovered that some of his claims didn't quite check out.

But even that would have been fine with Admiral Markcy, who was known to tell a story or two about his days as a Hollywood man-about-town when formal dinners at Calumet had moved to the stage of cigars and brandy in front of the fire.

In fact, the Admiral and the new owner undoubtedly would have hit it off famously, which would have pleased Mrs. Markey enormously. To her dying day, she doted on the Admiral, just as she doted on the farm.

Back at the Calumet cemetery, so far from the tent that you couldn't even hear the auctioneer's chant, a man strolling among the tombstones, among the legends, couldn't help but remember a spring day in 1978, the last time the Admiral and Mrs. Markey saw a Calumet horse run in person.

His name was Alydar, and in the 1980s he became Calumet's greatest sire since Bull Lea in the 1940s and '50s. But that spring he was a strong Kentucky Derby contender, the best to carry the farm's silks in two decades.

The Admiral and Mrs. Markey were both so feeble then that they hadn't been to the races in years. But on this special day, the running of the Blue Grass Stakes at Keeneland, track officials sent a station wagon to bring them to the

Billy Reed with Alydar and his groom/exercise rider, Charlie Rose, at Churchill Downs.

Admiral and Mrs. Gene Markey at Keeneland.

track and position them at the top of the stretch away from the crowd.

Mrs. Markey wore white gloves that day, just as the ladies always did in her time, and she stood there in the spring sunlight next to the Admiral, peering at Alydar as jockey Jorge Velasquez brought the big colt over so she could see him.

"Hello, my lady," said Velasquez, crooning softly to the old lady in the white gloves as he patted Alydar on the neck.

"Here is your baby. Don't he look pretty?"

A few minutes later, as the field turned for home, Alydar flashed past where the Markeys were standing, surging to the lead, a poem of power and motion in the devil's red and blue. He won that day by 13 lengths and the old lady left the track clutching the Blue Grass trophy in her white gloves.

Unfortunately for Alydar, he was runner-up to Affirmed in each of that year's Triple Crown races. Yet in defeat he acquired a sort of nobility that even his conqueror never achieved, mainly because Alydar was the Calumet horse that everybody loved.

So yesterday, leaving the Calumet cemetery after the auction, a man remembered that Blue Grass day at Keeneland. The new owner says he won't change a blade of grass, meaning the legends and their ghosts will remain undisturbed.

The Admiral and his lady in the white gloves would have liked the way the script ended. Their Old Kentucky Home had been saved.

Weep no more, indeed.

BUD DELP AND SPECTACULAR BID
"Go Bet On Him"

[From *The Courier-Journal*, April 1979]

Between now and Saturday afternoon, Grover G. "Bud" Delp probably will break all the Churchill Downs records for popping off and blowing up. He's so irreverent and outrageous that whenever he opens his mouth the twin spires shake and Kentucky colonels gag on their mint juleps. He's ready for the Kentucky Derby, but is the Derby ready for him?

The 47-year-old trainer is charming, amusing, witty and friendly. He's also obnoxious, tactless, childish and arrogant. The one thing he is not is dull. When he's not bragging on Spectacular Bid—"Hell, this horse is the biggest cinch I've had since I've been training," Delp says—he is doing something equally interesting, such as punching an exercise boy or tongue-lashing his jockey or attacking the racing establishment.

This week Delp will be the most heavily interviewed and closely watched man at the Downs. Spectacular Bid is the favorite for the 105th running of the Derby on Saturday, but he's coming off a confusing race in the Blue Grass Stakes at Keeneland. He won by seven lengths, maintaining his unbeaten record for this year, but his time of 1:50 for the mile and an eighth was terribly slow. The Blue Grass seemed to subdue Delp, but not for long. Yesterday, he was his usual buoyant self as he supervised Bid's installation in Barn 41 at the Downs. Nothing subdues Delp very long—more than anything, he's a survivor—so everyone can look forward to a week full of one-liners and boasts.

Billy Reed interviews trainer Buddy Delp on the backside of Belmont Park, 1979.

Most of the time Delp is funny, but every now and then there is a sharp edge to his comments. In a way, the cockiness is a mask for the insecurity and bitterness that still lurks in the recesses of his mind.

Like a lot of self-made men, Delp can never quite forget where he came from, or how hard it was to get to the top. So sometimes he can't resist the urge to get even for the slights, real or imagined, that he has suffered in 20 years of scuffling. Indeed, Delp seems to relish the idea that racing's bluebloods finally are forced to pay attention—and homage—to a guy who knows what it's like to be too broke to buy a hamburger.

How hard has it been for Delp?

His father drowned when he was only three years old, so his mother had to work as a secretary to support Bud and his brother. When Bud was nine, his mother married a horse trainer named Raymond Archer, and Archer introduced Bud to the race track.

As a kid in Belair, Maryland, Delp was sort of what used to be called a juvenile dilinquent. He spent his days setting pins in a bowling alley, his nights shooting pool.

"I played a lot of hookey, went to the races a lot," Delp said. "I climbed over fences and under fences. Used to tug on people's coattails to get the money for a $2 bet."

In 1955, Delp went to work for his stepfather. "I walked hots, ponied horses, groomed a little bit," Delp said. "I didn't like working in manure, but I did like the atmosphere of the race track."

His stepfather made him an assistant trainer in 1959. "I was the assistant trainer, but really I was the trainer," Delp said. "He'd come out on paydays and afternoons. He got the credit and I got broke. I used to carry an alarm clock in my car and sleep on the side of the turnpikes. And I was dead broke."

"I remember one night back in the fall of '62, I had to go from Delaware (Park) to Monmouth with six horses. I had barely enough gas in the car to make it and barely enough to buy one hamburger before I hit the turnpike. I told my stepfather that if I didn't get more money, I'd have to leave and he said, 'When are you leaving?' We parted company in '62."

The race track was the perfect forum for Delp's guts and guile. By 1965, Delp had proven his ability to claim horses and turn them into winners. To illustrate his ability to survive, Delp tells the story about what happened after he lost 30 of 32 horses in a fire at Laurel in '65.

"It was still smoking over there and I claimed three horses," Delp said. "A month later, I was the leading trainer at Pimlico."

His work with claiming horses was so impressive that, a few years ago, Delp finally began getting some good stock from Canadian sportsman Edward P. Taylor and others who race in Maryland. That was all Delp needed to prove his training savvy. Last year his stable won 226 races and $1.7 million in purses, making him the third leading trainer in the country. Among his good horses of recent years was Sweet Alliance, who won the Kentucky Oaks in 1977.

Besides Taylor, Delp also trains for nine other interests, including, of course, Hawksworth Farm, owner of Spectacular Bid. Hawksworth is owned by Harry Meyerhoff, a construction executive from Baltimore; his wife, Teresa, and his son, Tom. "I train for people that can afford the game," Delp says. "I don't want to train for no s.o.b. that says, 'Here's $10,000, make me some money.' I want him to say, 'Here's $10,000, let's have some fun.'"

Delp remembers how he got hooked up with the Meyerhoffs. "It was about 10 years ago," he said. "Harry approached me and I turned him down. I was loaded. He primarily wanted to go to the sale and buy young horses, and I was the top dog already in Maryland. He asked again a couple of years later, and this time I was interested."

On the advice of Delp, the Hawksworth owners—Harry, Teresa and Tom Meyerhoff—bought Bid for $37,000 in a yearling sale at Keeneland. "The Meyerhoffs go down there (to Keeneland) to have fun—and they do—and, dammit, that's what it's all about," Delp said. "They go to Keeneland three times a year, but that's enough. Harry puts on a show.

"They check the catalogs and get 150 or 200 horses to look at; then we start about 7:30 or 8 in the morning. I have the right to veto. I either like 'em or I don't. If I got a yes, then Harry goes to work.

"We liked Bid an awful lot. In fact, I think they were ready to go to 60 grand. We got him for $37,000, so they're already $23,000 ahead. Harry handed me the sales slip, like he always does, and said, 'Here's the next champion.' Then we went to the barn and had a drink. They're great."

Still, Delp didn't become nationally known until last year, when Spectacular Bid developed into the leading 2-year-old in America. The son of Bold Bidder locked up the juvenile championship—and established himself as the early Derby favorite—by demolishing his top rivals in the Laurel Futurity last fall.

Suddenly, everyone wanted to know all about Bud Delp, and Delp was only too happy to tell them. "I'm just happy to have this horse," he says. "You guys (reporters) are here talking to me now and I'm not doing anything different than I've been doing for 17 years. I'm not really a better trainer now than I ever was. Just a lot of people know it now. I like the exposure, I guess."

Most of the time, that is. When Bid comes out of the barn to train, the balderdash vanishes and Delp becomes tense. Last fall he punched out an exercise boy who brought his horse too close to Bid on the track. And if the track isn't in perfect condition, or if it's too crowded, Delp is apt to go into a tirade.

"In 20 years, I've seen everything happen to a horse," Delp says, "so I want to eliminate any hazards with this horse. If something happens to him, let it be out there on the track heading for that bull's-eye, and not some stupid act that could have been prevented by the groom, the exercise boy, the hotwalker, even me. I'm not worried about anything, but I'm worried about Spectacular Bid all the time."

Delp's detractors are seizing upon the Blue Grass to make the argument that Bid isn't sharp enough to beat Flying Paster, king of the West Coast. If they're right, Delp will be roasted for everything from working Bid too hard to using young jockey Ronnie Franklin to bragging too much. But Delp, the survivor, is ready for whatever life deals.

"If I'm wrong, they won't get a maiden," Delp has said. "I've been wrong more than most and right more than most. If that horse (Paster) is as good as Secretariat, Derby Day you're going to see a horse race."

[Epilogue: On Derby Day, as he followed Bid from the barn area to the paddock, Delp yelled, "Go bet! Go bet!" Bid won the Derby and Preakness, but finished third in the Belmont, at least partly because a safety pin had been lodged in one of his feet. As a four-year-old in 1980, Bid was the unbeaten Horse of the Year. Typically, Delp called him "the greatest horse ever to look through a bridle."]

JOHN CAMPO
"The Fat Man"

[The Churchill Downs website, January 2003]

The straw who stirred the mint julep at the 1981 Kentucky Derby was John Campo, the cocky, feisty New Yorker who packed 250 pounds on his 5'7" frame, not counting the huge chip on his shoulder, and liked to call himself "The Fat Man," as in, "This horse is going to win the Triple Crown . . . Hey, the Fat Man tells you something, you go to sleep on it."

He said that only moments after Pleasant Colony, the ugly-duckling colt he trained for Thomas Mellon Evans' Buckland Farm of Virginia, had made good on Campo's guarantee that he would win the Wood Memorial at Aqueduct. Despite being so skinny that his ribs showed and a slow-healing chemical burn on his left hindquarters, the son of His Majesty, out of the mare Sun Colony, won the Wood by three lengths.

"Bleeping easy, that's what it was," said Campo as he paced around, waiting for jockey Jeff Fell to bring Pleasant Colony back to the winner's circle at Aqueduct. "And we're going to Kentucky and beat those bleepity bleeps, too."

That set the tone for a rowdy, raucous Triple Crown in which The Fat Man loudly insulted rival trainers, scoffed at the competition, and even got into a heated exchange with former riding great Eddie Arcaro, then working for ABC, that almost ended in a fistfight at a Baltimore restaurant.

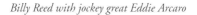

Billy Reed with jockey great Eddie Arcaro

Pleasant Colony wears the garland of roses after winning the 1981 Kentucky Derby. That's jockey Jorge Velasquez aboard.

Pleasant Colony, who died on Tuesday, Dec. 31, 2002 at the Blue Ridge Farm in Upperville, Virginia, was Campo's horse of a lifetime. After he finished a dull fifth in the 1981 Florida Derby, owner Evans took him away from trainer Phil O'Donnell Lee on March 16 and turned him over to Campo.

Evans apparently was angry with Lee for running the colt despite a fever and the burns on his left hindquarters, which resulted from a chemical being overturned in his stall. His new trainer, Campo, had never won a Triple Crown race. Moreover, he was several furlongs removed from the patrician Evans in temperament, taste, and social standing.

So, after the Wood Memorial, in which Pleasant Colony upset 1-5 favorite Cure the Blues, it was amusing to see Campo in the winner's circle, nudging Mellon in the ribs and saying, "O.K., boss, did I do all right?"

Campo, who was then 43, quit school at 16 so he could go to work on the racetrack. He worked for some of the game's best—Sunny Jim Fitzsimmons, John Nerud, Lucien Laurin, and Eddie Neloy—before striking out on his own in 1968.

Although Campo developed such outstanding horses as Jim French (second in the 1970 Derby), Protagonist, and Talking Picture, he never lost his underdog's mentality. He felt that the "society trainers" who worked for the establishment stables looked down their noses at him. To them, he would always be only a working-class, Italian-American from Queens.

After the Wood, Campo lashed out at the handiest target, Frank Wright, a "society trainer" who was doing the TV commentary for ABC. When Wright said that Cure the Blues was the only good horse in the race, Campo bristled. He lashed back after the race.

"Where's Frank Wright?" he yelled. "Only one good horse in the race, huh? Yeah, and Campo's got him! Campo's got him! Knock my horse . . . Frank Wright oughta be selling papers. All these fancy trainers . . . hey, the Fat Man's got a horse."

Unconvinced, Bert Firestone, the owner of Cure the Blues, decided to try Pleasant Colony in the Derby. The field also included Proud Appeal, a colt that impressed Lexington breeder John Gaines so much in winning the Blue Grass Stakes that Gaines forked over $5 million for a half-interest in him; Partez, the first Derby entrant for trainer D. Wayne Lukas; and Woodchopper, from the famed Greentree Stable and respected trainer John M. Gaver, Jr.

Although Campo would later boast that Pleasant Colony "won easy," that really wasn't the case on May 3 at Churchill Downs.

Coming from 17th place in the 21-horse field, Pleasant Colony, with regular jockey Jorge Velasquez back in the irons, made a big move on the backstretch and in the turn for home, sweeping to the lead as the field headed down the long stretch.

But instead of winning more or less under wraps, as he had in the Wood, Pleasant Colony was fully extended to hold off Woodchopper, whose late charge came up short by only three-quarters of a length.

After the race, in which jockey Sandy Hawley misjudged the finish line aboard the third-place Partez, Campo didn't make fun of Proud Appeal (14th) and Cure the Blues (15th), but he did make sure that he, not jockey Velasquez, got credit for the victory.

"I put no bouquets on Velasquez," Campo said. "He knows, as crazy as I am, that I'd take him off this horse tomorrow. But he did a super, super job today."

As Pleasant Colony was being led back to the barns after the Derby, he became the first and only Derby winner to have his roses stolen. A hustler wearing a policeman's uniform grabbed the garland of roses from Campo's son, John Jr., and said that he would carry them to the barn.

"When I looked around again," said the younger Campo, "he was gone."

"That's terrible," said Campo, who found out the hard way that he hadn't learned all the cons and scams growing up in Queens.

On the Thursday night before the Preakness in Baltimore, Campo attended a Pimlico-sponsored "crabfest" at Captain Harvey's near the track.

While "The Fat Man" was demonstrating why he deserved his nickname, Arcaro arrived and sat down at Campo's table. As he was stuffing himself with crabs, Campo began to taunt Arcaro about picking Cure the Blues to win both the Wood and the Derby.

It wasn't long before they were on their feet, shouting at each other. When Arcaro accused Campo of being a bad trainer, Campo challenged him to name one better. Arcaro threw out the name of Buddy Hirsch, the son of famed trainer Max Hirsch, and Campo offered to bet Arcaro $10,000 that he had more stakes wins than Hirsch.

The bet quickly escalated from $10,000 to $100,000. Campo demanded that Arcaro whip out $100,000 from his pocket and put it on the table. Arcaro said he didn't have that much on him, but could get it by morning. Then he tried to get Campo to put the bet in writing.

Just when it seemed that punches would be thrown, cooler heads pulled the two apart. Campo and his group left, but not before The Fat Man darkly vowed to "embarrass" Arcaro, who hung around to drink and insult Campo to whomever would listen.

At the next day's Alibi Breakfast, Arcaro picked Partez to beat Pleasant Colony. "Aw, that's just because of what happened Thursday night," Campo said. "He's an adult, but he's a kid. I embarrassed him and insulted him and he can't handle it. Arcaro's a complete ass. He wouldn't know a racehorse if you put one in front of him."

Strong words, considering that Arcaro won the Triple Crown with Whirlaway in 1941 and Citation in '48. But Arcaro also wasn't backing down. "Campo's a bad trainer," Arcaro said. "He's just gotten lucky with one decent horse."

In the Preakness, that "decent horse" gave The Fat Man gloating rights. Once again he came from off the pace, hooked Bold Ego in the stretch, and gradually drew away for a one-length victory. Partez finished fifth and Woodchopper 11th.

As pleased as he was with Pleasant Colony's victory, Campo was almost as thrilled by the demise of Partez, the colt Arcaro had picked. Along the way, Campo also had referred to Lukas, the colt's trainer, as a "nitwit."

"They oughta ship that horse back to California," Campo said. (They did, rather than try Pleasant Colony again in the Belmont.)

Wisely, ABC didn't assign Arcaro to interview Campo. "I undressed him," Campo said. "They don't respect The Fat Man, but I don't care. Hey, I'm a great trainer. I can make a horse do anything I want. I tell the jock what to do and he better listen." (By the way, Campo would have won the bet with Arcaro. At the time, he had 63 stakes winners; Buddy Hirsch retired with 55.)

Back at the Pimlico stakes barn, Campo lashed out at columnist Dick

Young of the *New York Daily News*, who had written about the ugly rash on Pleasant Colony's right hindquarters.

"I don't talk about your wife and kids," Campo said to Young.

"My wife didn't run in the Preakness," Young replied.

"Hey, I don't want anybody talking about my property," Campo said.

"John," Young said, "the rash is all over his ass."

"That's your opinion, Dick," Campo fired back. "Don't put me down. Ain't nobody's business what it is."

Actually, the colt's appearance was a fact, not Young's opinion. "He's not a good-looking horse," said Jack Van Berg, trainer of runnerup Bold Ego. "I like Johnny and all that, but I gotta be truthful with you. He's not anything that you would want to look at."

"He is not going to win the halter class," said Lukas, using a show-horse term that applies to horses with good conformation. "He's lop-eared, coarse, and gangly, but he also has a good stride and a nice shoulder. The main thing is, he's the horse that gets the money."

Although Campo predicted that the Belmont Stakes would be "a piece of cake . . . like taking candy from a baby," he also made it clear that Pleasant Colony didn't need to win the Triple Crown to certify his ability as a trainer.

"It doesn't make any difference," Campo said. "Lucien Laurin (trainer of Secretariat) and Billy Turner (trainer of Seattle Slew) won the Triple Crown and they got fired. Hey, you know what they do with old newspapers? They throw them away. I know what kind of ability I got. That's all that matters."

But Greentree's Gaver, citing all the traffic problems that hurt his colt in both the Derby and Preakness, said he thought the Belmont might turn into Woodchopper's Ball.

"I still think I should have beaten him in Louisville," Gaver said. "And in the Preakness, considering the luck we had, I couldn't have beat a stable pony. I'll have to have one more crack at him."

At the post-position draw and breakfast the Thursday before the Belmont, Campo hammed it up with Mickey Rooney, the actor who then was starring in "Sugar Babes" on Broadway. As a kid growing up in California, Rooney worked on the track as an exercise boy. Once, he even worked out the great Seabiscuit.

"He's a Cinderella man," said Rooney, hugging Campo. "He's not only a great trainer, he's a great showman."

In the Belmont, however, the lights went out for The Fat Man.

Turning for home in the mile-and-a-half classic, Pleasant Colony had dead aim on the front-running Summing and Highland Blade. But this time, the colt didn't respond when Velasquez asked. He finished third, a length behind Highland Blade, who lost a photo finish with Summing.

"I tried my best," said Velasquez. "I rode him the same as I did in the Derby and Preakness. We don't have any excuses."

Neither did Gaver, whose Woodchopper was fourth, 11 lengths behind Pleasant Colony. Pleasant Colony, Woodchopper, and Bold Ego were the only three horses to dance all the Triple Crown dances. Bold Ego, the Preakness runner-up, was last in the 11-horse Belmont field.

Surprisingly, Campo was gracious in defeat.

"He flat got beat and that was it," Campo said. "You can't knock him for getting beat. He didn't get beat that bad. It's part of the game, that's all."

That fall, Pleasant Colony won the Woodward Stakes at Belmont, but was retired to stud after a fourth-place finish in the Marlboro Cup. He left the track with six wins, three seconds and his Belmont third to show for 14 career starts. He won the Eclipse Award given to the nation's best 3-year-old colt.

"He no look like a race horse," said Luis Barrera, training of Summing, "but he run like a race horse."

Pleasant Colony began his breeding career at Buckland Farm, and in 1998 was shifted to Lane's End Farm in Kentucky. In 2000, at age 22, he was pensioned and moved to Blue Ridge Farm.

Among his 73 stakes winners were Pleasant Tap, third in the 1990 Derby, and Pleasant Stage; European star St. Jovite; 1993 Belmont winner Colonial Affair; and recent handicap star Behrens.

The Fat Man, who never won another Triple Crown race, retired in the early 1990s after suffering a stroke.

WOODY STEPHENS
A Long Way From Midway

[From the *Lexington Herald-Leader*, August 1998]

On the day of the 1984 Kentucky Derby, Woody Stephens was not in good shape. He had just been released from the hospital, where he had been treated for pneumonia complicated by emphysema and broken ribs suffered in a bathroom fall.

So Churchill Downs president Lynn Stone worked it out so Stephens, who was training Swale for Claiborne Farm, could be brought from his motel to the track, where he was escorted through the crowd to the directors' room to watch the Derby on TV.

I was standing next to him, and as Swale took the lead in the turn for home, Woody nudged me and said, "They're not going to catch him today, Bill. He's going to win by five."

For the record, the official margin was 3-1/4 lengths. It was one of Woody's favorite wins because it was the first Derby victory for Claiborne, long a pillar of Kentucky's world-famous breeding establishment.

When the race was over, Woody hardly looked like the sick man he was.

Suddenly he was all wrinkles, crinkles and twinkles, cackling at putting over another one at the highest level of the game.

When Stephens died yesterday [8/22/98], nine days short of his 85th birthday, racing lost one of its greatest horsemen and most endearing characters. I can see him now on the rain-soaked afternoon of June 7, 1986, leading Danzig Connection—his record fifth consecutive Belmont winner—into the winner's

71

circle at Belmont Park while the crowd chanted "Wood-ee, Wood-ee."

Later, in the press box, Stephens engaged in his favorite activity—talking about himself—while holding a glass of Scotch ("That champagne will rot your brain," he said) and showing off the red necktie that the Fasig-Tipton sales company had given him for luck.

"He was the best-looking horse in the race and the best-trained horse in the race," Stephens cracked in that cocky way that somehow always managed to be far more charming than annoying.

It was always easy to forgive Woody his pride. He came up the hard way, the son of a tobacco farmer from Stanton. As he said after winning the l00th Kentucky Derby with Cannonade in 1974, "We never had much, and I've worked hard for everything I got."

At the time he was 60, a little late to be reaching his prime, but for the next 15 years, largely because of his association with Claiborne and Henryk de Kwiatkowski, Woody was one of the game's major players.

He became known as "the artful codger."

The five consecutive Belmont winners will stand forever as a tribute to Woody's horsemanship because each was beset by one problem or another.

• In 1982 Woody treated Conquistador Cielo with a special electromagnetic "boot" to get him ready for his 14-length Belmont win, only five days after he had scored a stunning triumph in the Metropolitan Mile.

• In '83, jockey Laffit Pincay Jr. almost was knocked through the rail before finding enough running room for Caveat to prevail.

• Eight days before dying of an apparent heart attack in 1984, Claiborne's Swale bounced back from a poor Preakness showing to add the Belmont to his Derby triumph.

• In '85, Stephens shocked everyone by running 1-2 in the Belmont with the gelding Creme Fraiche and Stephan's Odyssey.

• Danzig Connection won the Belmont after coming back from bone chips in a knee. Owner de Kwiatkowski was amazed by Woody's magic. "I thought," he said, "that if he couldn't win an allowance race, how could he win the Belmont Stakes?"

Woody's last hurrah came a decade ago, when Forty Niner, a colt he trained for Claiborne, barely missed catching Winning Colors, the roan filly trained by D. Wayne Lukas, in the 114th Derby.

Two weeks later, after the Preakness, jockey Gary Stevens accused Stephens of poor sportsmanship during the race won by Risen Star.

Stevens claimed Stephens ordered jockey Pat Day to interfere with Winning Colors, a charge Woody vehemently denied.

"Wayne called me later with Charlsie Cantey (of ABC-TV)," said Stephens, "and he said, 'Woody didn't do anything that I wouldn't have done.'

I appreciated that."

Even as you read this, I'm certain Woody is standing at the Pearly Gates, showing St. Peter the wristwatch the New York Racing Association gave him for winning his five consecutive Belmonts.

"See this watch?" he'll be saying, with a cackle. "The only way Lukas will get one like this is if I leave it to him."

Well, I'm confident that when Woody's will is read, he won't leave the watch to Lukas, his training rival in the 1970s and '80s. But I hope they don't bury it with him because it belongs in the Kentucky Derby Museum, where Woody is one of the main narrators in the video that's played repeatedly every day.

As long as Woody's on that recording, we won't have to rely on memory alone to recall his voice, his laugh, and, mostly, his love for horses and the hopes and dreams they represent.

For 24 years, I spent a lot of enjoyable hours talking with Stephens. We talked in the morning at the barns, in the afternoons after some of his biggest wins and at nights over cocktails and dinner. We also had plenty of phone conversations.

So I've culled my files to come up with a list of what I'll call "Woodyisms." Long before Bob Baffert came along—or even D. Wayne Lukas—Stephens was a guy who never met a notebook or a tape recorder he didn't like.

• On jockey Eddie Arcaro's view of his career: "Arcaro told me once that the greatest thing that ever happened to me was to find out I couldn't ride."

• On Manny Ycaza, who rode for Stephens when he was training Cain Hoy Stable for Capt. Harry Guggenheim in the 1950s and '60s: "He was just a fireball. He was the kind of rider who always gave 100 percent. And if he didn't feel that he was riding at his best, he would just take off in the middle of the day and leave."

• On Believe It, a mudder who finished third to Affirmed and Alydar in the 1978 Kentucky Derby: "A lot of horses don't accept the mud. Others seem to be bred for it. I can almost read the pedigree and tell you whether a horse is going to be a mudder or not."

• On Smarten, the colt with whom he won six consecutive stakes races in 1979 while ducking Spectacular Bid and other stars: "He's won on big tracks and he's won at bullrings. He's won on the grass, in the slop, on heavy tracks and lightning-fast tracks. Where he's been, doing what he's done, you got to say he's a good horse."

• On the Saratoga meeting: "I like it here, but it's tiresome, awful tiresome. Years ago, they said that if you survived Saratoga, then you'd survive the year."

• After winning his first Belmont Stakes with Conquistador Cielo in

73

1982: "How good can it get? I came up here as a country boy. Had an eighth-grade education. The game's been good to me. Something like this doesn't excite me like it did a long time ago. But I still like to win races."

• After winning his second Belmont with Caveat in 1983: "When they run like this, it's hard to walk away, isn't it?"

•After winning his third Belmont with Claiborne Farm's Swale in 1984: "This is a lovely race to win; I'd like to do it again next year."

• After Creme Fraiche and Stephan's Odyssey ran one-two in the 1985 Belmont: "I think that this possibly is the best thing that's ever happened to me in my life."

• To the media after Danzig Connection gave him his fifth consecutive Belmont in 1986: "See you next year. Same time. Be here."

• Before trying to get his first Travers Stakes with Danzig Connection: "I'd like to win it, but I never think much about it. It's the kind of thing that if I won, I'd wake up Sunday and think, 'That was nice.' But it wouldn't be like going through a career without winning the Kentucky Derby or the Belmont. Compared to those, the Travers is just another race."

• After winning his first Travers with Claiborne's Forty Niner in 1988: "We've won a lot of big ones, and it's great to win this one. This horse is as game as they come. He'll fight you back."

• On whether it's tougher to win five consecutive Belmonts or five consecutive Triple Crown races: "Oh, hell, five Belmonts in a row stands out. Anybody can win 'em all over the country. It's something just to have a starter in five straight Belmonts, much less win all of them."

CHARLIE WHITTINGHAM AND BILL SHOEMAKER
The Sunshine Boys

[From *The Courier-Journal*, May 1986]

The soft morning light was washing over the tiny man in the red jacket, and all around him were the smells and sounds of horses. This, said Bill Shoemaker, smiling, was the elixir that keeps him young at 54.

He was standing outside Barn 41 at Churchill Downs, waiting to go have breakfast with trainer Charlie Whittingham. Only 4 feet 11 and 95 pounds, he was still the biggest man around.

You don't measure The Shoe's stature in inches or pounds or even years. You measure it in wins (more than 8,600) and earnings (more than $100 million) and memories.

He rode his first Kentucky Derby in 1952, when Harry S. Truman was in the White House. Three times he has won the roses on the first Saturday in May. When he climbs aboard Ferdinand Saturday afternoon, he'll stretch his record for Derby mounts to 24.

So when Shoemaker is of a mind to talk about horses past and horses present, as he was there yesterday under the morning sun, a humble listener pays close attention.

A tight smile flitting on his lips. The Shoe yesterday told a story about the 1965 Derby, when he left a party at 4:30 a.m. Friday and came straight to Churchill to work out a horse while still wearing his tuxedo and patent-leather shoes.

The horse, fortunately, wasn't Lucky Debonair, which Shoemaker that

75

year rode to his third—and most recent—Derby victory.

"It was so cold that night I just about froze my tail off," Shoemaker said, "and I couldn't see from here to there. All I could think of was, 'What are you doing on this horse?' It would have made a great picture."

So, of course, would the sight of Ferdinand and his Sunshine Boys, Shoemaker and Whittingham, in the winner's circle late Saturday afternoon after the 112th Run for the Roses.

Neither Shoemaker, who has failed only to ride a Triple Crown winner, nor trainer Whittingham, the 73-year-old "Bald Eagle" of American racing, would be in Louisville this week if he didn't think Ferdinand had a great chance to win.

Consider this: Whittingham swore after training Divine Comedy to a ninth-place finish in 1960 that he would never again come to the Derby unless he was going to win it all.

"Yep, that's me," Whittingham admits. "The Derby is a great race to win, but it's also the biggest baloney race there is because of all the sports writers who might not see another race all year."

Indeed, Whittingham hasn't received the national recognition that belongs to, say, Woody Stephens or Laz Barrera or even D. Wayne Lukas because he never has saddled the winner of a Triple Crown race (Derby, Preakness, and Belmont Stakes).

But he has made a fortune by being patient with his young horses, letting the Triple Crown contenders fall by the wayside, and then cleaning up on the major stakes, mostly in California, with older horses.

"You've seen that old adage, 'Pay me now or pay me later?' Well, that's me," Whittingham says. "Woody keeps track of all his stakes wins, but I've got more to do. I'm a hard worker. And I've been lucky for a guy born on April 13, 1913."

More than lucky. A trainer since 1932, Whittingham has won more $100,000 races than any other trainer, been seven times the national leader in earnings, and trained more than 40 horses to major stakes wins, including Ack Ack, Cougar II, Perrault and Kennedy Road.

His hair began to fall out when be contracted malaria in 1945 while serving with the Marines in the Pacific Theater, so he began shaving his head long before Yul Brynner or Telly Savalas.

Even now, Whittingham smiles at the memory of Santa Anita track announcer Joe Hernandez, who used to delight in introducing him as "The baaaaalllllddd eagle from the Sierra Madres!"

Many of Whittingham's stakes winners have been owned by Howard Keck, who bred Ferdinand and runs the colt in the name of his wife, Elizabeth. After Keck inherited Superior Oil Co. from his father, it was sold to Mobil in

1984 for $5.7 billion.

A son of Nijinksy II, Ferdinand has Derby winners in both sides of his family tree. His paternal grandfather is Northern Dancer, winner of the 1964 Derby, while his dam, Banja Luka, is a granddaughter of 1953 Derby winner Dark Star.

While Ferdinand has only two wins to show for nine career starts, his record this year—all in California stakes—shows a head loss to Badger Land in the Los Feliz, a win in the Santa Catalina, a close second to Variety Road in the San Rafael, and a distant third to Snow Chief and Icy Groom in the Santa Anita Derby.

"In the Santa Anita Derby, where the track was kind of wet-fast, he was slipping all the way," Whittingham said. "Those little digging horses do a lot better on that kind of track. Ferdinand is a very big, long-striding horse."

But what Whittingham really likes about Ferdinand is that The Shoe fits. While conceding that Shoemaker may not quite be the rider he used to be, Whittingham also believes that his jockey still ranks among the best in the business. "Shoe's riding very well now," Whittingham said. "He's smarter now. And he has been around this track so many times that he'll know where he's going in the Derby."

After making his debut aboard Count Flame in 1952, Shoemaker's Derby wins came aboard Swaps in 1955, Tomy Lee in '59 and Lucky Debonair (sans tuxedo and patent-leather shoes) in '65.

He also would have had the roses aboard Gallant Man in '57, had he not misjudged the finish line and stood up in the irons just long enough to let Bill Hartack get past with Iron Leige. Third was Round Table.

Yesterday Shoemaker and Hartack were chatting outside Barn 41 when a bystander said, "I saw old Round Table at the farm the other day. He's 32 now and so's Gallant Man."

If memories of the '57 Derby flashed into the minds of either Shoemaker or Hartack, each kept his own counsel. Instead, Hartack, the winner of five Derbies, changed the subject. "I thought your best Derby horse was Tomy Lee," Hartack said, "because he was so hard to ride."

Shoemaker nodded. "Yeah he was a tough horse," he said. "He wanted to lay on that side all the time."

In 1964, Hartack again was the beneficiary of a mistake in judgment by Shoemaker, who had the mount on Northern Dancer but switched to Hill Rise just before the Keeneland meeting.

On Derby Day, Hartack and Northern Dancer outlasted Shoemaker and Hill Rise in a thrilling stretch duel that retired steward Jack Goode rates as the best be ever saw.

Now here's Shoemaker on a grandson of Northern Dancer, trying to accomplish in the Derby something akin to what another graybeard, 46-year-old golfer Jack Nicklaus, did recently in the Masters.

"Yeah, that gave me a little hope there," said Shoemaker, making a fist and pumping it in the air. "This just might the year of the older guys."

His tuxedoed escapade before the '65 Derby notwithstanding, Shoemaker obviously has taken rather good care of his body. This year, be said, he began doing daily push-ups, chin-ups, sit-ups and stretching exercises to keep limber.

Asked about retirement, Shoemaker will only shrug and smile.

"I've been trying to retire for 15 years," he said, "but I've never gotten around to it. I was thinking about it when I was 36 or 37. But when it got right down to it, I couldn't do it."

Now he's 54 and still hoping to smell the roses one more time. But even if he doesn't, it was at least nice to stand there in the soft morning light of Churchill Downs and again share a few moments with this giant of a man named Shoemaker.

[Epilogue: In the Derby, Ferdinand seemed hopelessly trapped behind a wall of traffic as the field turned for home. Spying a small hole on the rail, Shoemaker sent Ferdinand through it, and the colt rolled on to a 2 1/4-length victory. Some experts believe it was Shoemaker's greatest ride.]

D. WAYNE LUKAS
"My Turn, My Turn"

[From the *Lexington Herald-Leader*, May 1998]

Only a few minutes before post time for the 114th Kentucky Derby, trainer D. Wayne Lukas eased into the track superintendent's office just off the chute leading out to the Churchill Downs track.

Wearing his trademark tinted glasses and a dark blue suit, Lukas had just sent out the gray filly Winning Colors to test the colts in the world's most famous horse race, the Kentucky Derby.

"She went out there perfectly dry," Lukas said. "She danced all the way over, with the crowd raising hell and all, but she never turned a hair and went out there perfectly."

He paced back and forth, sometimes stopping to glance at his program. Otherwise, he hid his butterflies well, especially for a man facing what was, arguably, the most important race of his illustrious career.

Surely even little old ladies in Dubuque, Iowa, have heard tell of D. Wayne Lukas, the former basketball coach and quarter horse trainer who exploded into thoroughbred racing nine years ago, and proceeded to corner the market on wins, earnings and Derby futility.

Going into yesterday's race, he had run 12 horses in the last 7 Derbies, never finishing better than third. No trainer in history had run more horses without smelling the roses.

He had tried everything—big horses and little ones, bays and grays, front-runners and late-kickers, colts and fillies, horses running alone and in entries.

Nothing had worked—but also, nothing had shaken his enormous confidence in himself, his system and his stable. Every year, on the day after the Derby, Lukas makes motel reservations for next year as he checks out. His relentless pursuit of the roses, coupled with his enormous confidence and enormous success, has earned Lukas his share of critics and enemies, some of whom contended that he would never win a Derby because he was too hard on his horses.

But those individuals didn't happen to be at his barn on the morning after the 1983 Derby—a morning on which Lukas' mood was a perfect match for the gloomy, cold, drizzly weather.

Once again he had come up short, this time with a three-horse entry (Marfa, Balboa Native and Total Departure) that had been the Derby favorite. As he worked around the barn, Lukas couldn't help but second-guess himself. He broke his train of thought when a writer friend introduced him to a little girl, maybe 11 years old, who was in love with horses, particularly a special filly named Landaluce.

Trained by Lukas, Landaluce was unbeaten in 1982 when she suddenly became ill and died, despite the efforts of the best veterinarians Lukas could find. When she took her last breath, her head was in Lukas' arms.

So on that cold gray morning after the 1983 Derby, this slip of a girl met Lukas and didn't mention what had happened the previous day. All she said was, "I loved Landaluce."

At that, D. Wayne Lukas began to weep. He gently took the girl in his arms and hugged her, rocking slowly. This was the scene for a minute or so—a very long, very private, very touching minute.

Right then, the loquacious Lukas was more eloquent that he has ever been in any of his interviews. As he let out all the pent-up love and frustration and hurt, he spoke volumes about why he's in the game.

"I knew then that I'd be all right," Lukas would recall last week. "I knew then that the little girl's love for a horse is what this game is all about—and what makes the hurt worthwhile."

Now here he was five years later, standing in this little office outside the chute at Churchill Downs and fidgeting about another filly.

As he waited, Lukas kept his thoughts to himself. Just before the start, he exchanged a few comments with John Campo Jr., who was helping his father train Intensive Command.

"I got the only gray in the race," Lukas said. "We'll find her."

"I know where I'll be," said the young Campo.

The start of the Kentucky Derby was only moments away, and now

Trainer D. Wayne Lukas being interviewed by Billy Reed.

Lukas was left to review his feelings, his plans and his decisions.

Going into the year, as usual, the Lukas barn was brimming with Derby contenders. He had won last year's $1 million Breeders' Cup Juvenile with Success Express. He also had Tejano, Cougarized, Tsarbaby, Notebook and Dynaformer. But as the year wore on and the prep races unfolded, Lukas gradually eliminated one colt after another as he began thinking more and more seriously about running Winning Colors in the Kentucky Derby instead of the Kentucky Oaks. When Eugene V. Klein's daughter of the imported stallion Caro went wire-to-wire while scoring a powerful 7-1/2-length victory over colts in the April 9 Santa Anita Derby, she earned her trip to Kentucky.

"I know I'll probably be criticized for running a filly against colts," said Lukas afterward, "but all the women in America will be screaming at me if I don't. And I think they would be right. This was the most impressive Derby prep race of any horse I've ever had."

So Lukas, typically, did what he felt was right, even though he well knew that only two fillies in 113 years—Regret in 1915 and Genuine Risk in 1980—had been strong enough to beat the colts over a mile and a quarter on the first Saturday in May.

Even more audacious, he eventually decided to skip the Derby with all his colts—and never mind that Tejano had won more than $1 million, Notebook had run tough against the respected Forty Niner in Florida, and Dynaformer had thrown in a big win in New York.

The skeptics couldn't help but wonder if Lukas was making the same mistake he made in 1984, when he became the first trainer to run two fillies in the same Derby. Sent off as the favorites in the 19-horse field, Life's Magic finished eighth and Althea last.

But Lukas felt that Winning Colors was different. Bigger, stronger and tougher than his '84 fillies, Winning Colors figured to benefit enormously from the fact that fillies have to carry only 121 pounds in the Derby, 5 fewer than the colts.

Now, finally, it was post time for the Derby, and Lukas moved closer to the television as the field sprang out of the starting gate late on what had been a hot, sunny afternoon.

As expected, Winning Colors went straight to the lead from her No. 11 post position. But instead of pressuring her into the first turn, the other riders were content to let her go while gaining position somewhere back in the pack. Sweeping out of the turn and heading down the backstretch, the filly looked relaxed on the lead, just as she had in the Santa Anita Derby.

"Stretch your legs, baby," Lukas said, letting his breath out slowly.

As the field left the backstretch and moved into the final turn, Lukas was so riveted to the TV that he began talking to jockey Gary Stevens.

Before the race, Lukas and Stevens had analyzed the day's races and noted that horses opening big leads at the top of the stretch were holding on to win. That, they decided, would be their strategy.

So as the TV showed Winning Colors sweeping into the turn, Lukas said, "Go ahead, Gary. . . . Go ahead. . . . C'mon, Gary, c'mon."

As the field turned for home, the filly had opened almost a four-length lead on the charging Proper Reality, who was barely ahead of Forty Niner and jockey Pat Day.

Only an eighth of a mile from the finish, Lukas yelled, "Switch leads, baby," meaning that it was time for Winning Colors to shift her lead leg, which usually helps horses shift into a higher gear.

As she galloped toward the wire, Forty Niner began to close ground. In the final strides, with the Claiborne colt getting ever closer, Lukas said, "Stay with it, Gary. . . . Stay with it, stay with it, stay with it."

When Winning Colors hit the finish line in front, a jubilant Lukas spun, slapped a friend on the back and shouted, "My turn . . . my turn!" as he headed out the door and into the chute, where he ran into the arms of some of his grooms.

"Boss, boss, we won it!" screamed a groom, grabbing Lukas in a bear hug.

"Where's Sherri?" asked Lukas, looking for his wife.

Here she came, tears streaming. After a hug and a kiss on the cheek for his wife, Lukas then whirled and hugged his son Jeff, also his top assistant and the trainer who worked with Winning Colors on a day-to-day basis.

Then he dashed out on the track, where he paused to give a couple of comments to reporters before heading on up the track to greet Stevens and the filly upon their triumphant return.

When the winning team finally drew near, Lukas reached across the rump of an intrusive stable pony to grab Stevens' outstretched hand.

"What a pretty race," he said, grinning broadly as the entire group began drifting toward the infield presentation stand.

And so did D. Wayne Lukas join the list of Kentucky Derby winners. Watching him smile, a fellow couldn't help but remember a cold morning long ago when the trainer embraced a little girl and wept for dreams lost, hopes faded and chances gone.

But as Lukas today would be the first to tell you, that sort of heartache only makes it that much sweeter when it's finally your turn to smell the roses in Kentucky on the first Saturday in May.

ARTHUR HANCOCK
The Prodigal Son

[From the Churchill Downs Website, August 2002]

Only a few in the Churchill Downs crowd of 122,653 realized they were watching more than a horse race when Sunday Silence and Easy Goer met for the first time in the 115th Kentucky Derby on May 6, 1989. The drama within the drama involved two families that were pillars of the racing establishment, an old grudge, and whether vindication could triumph over entitlement.

Sunday Silence, who was 17 when he died on Monday in Japan, was bred by Oak Cliff Stud and raised by Arthur Hancock III at his Stone Farm near Paris, Kentucky. In 1982, Hancock had become the first member of his famed family to win the Derby when the longshot Gato Del Sol came from last place in the 19-horse field to earn the roses.

Now he was back with a nearly-black son of Halo that had overcome conformation flaws and a serious illness to become a serious Derby contender for Hancock and his partners, trainer Charlie Whittingham and Dr. Ernest Gaillard.

However, despite an 11-length victory in the Santa Anita Derby, Sunday Silence still received second billing at Churchill Downs. The star was Easy Goer, the majestic son of Alydar who was being hyped as the sport's next superstar by the adoring New York media.

Easy Goer was bred and owned by Ogden Phipps, the 80-year-old financier whose high-class stable had won almost every race worth winning

Arthur Hancock with Billy Reed at Stone Farm.

except the Kentucky Derby. But now it looked as if Phipps' time finally had come. Trained beautifully by Lexington native Claude R. "Shug" McGaughey, Easy Goer came to Louisville off an impressive win in the Wood Memorial, his seventh victory in nine starts.

But Hancock, who liked to write country songs in his spare time (Sunday Silence's name came from Kris Kristofferson's "Sunday Morning Comin' Down"), felt strongly that he had poetic justice on his side. And as he privately told friends, nothing would make him happier than to ruin Phipps' dream.

When Arthur graduated from Vanderbilt University in 1965, he had a playboy's reputation and a musician's soul, neither of which endeared him to his father, A.B. "Bull" Hancock of the famed Claiborne Farm. So to give his elder son a sense of stability, Bull Hancock prevailed on Ogden Phipps, a friend since the 1940s, to give Arthur a summer job as a groom in New York.

At the time, Phipps' trainer was Eddie Neloy, a big and tough man who didn't take it easy on his new groom just because he was Bull Hancock's son. To the contrary, he ordered his stable foreman, an aspiring trainer named John Campo, to make life miserable for the playboy.

Of his $68-per-week salary, Arthur had to set aside $12 per week for a room in a boarding house near Belmont Park. It was a far cry from the mansion at Claiborne Farm, but there was one thing that made Arthur feel right at home. "I'd play my guitar up there and the landlord would tell me to shut up," Arthur said. "He didn't like the music, just like my dad. I remember the first time I played the guitar on the Paris radio station. I came home and dad just said, 'Well, here comes the canary home to roost.' I was so proud and he shot me right down."

When Arthur was lugging muck sacks, Phipps' son, Dinny, sometimes would drop by the barn with a limo and a couple of fashion models. Embarrassed, Arthur nevertheless hung in there just to prove to his father and the elder Phipps that they couldn't break his spirit.

When Bull Hancock died in 1972, the conditions of his will named Phipps, Charlie Kenney, and William Haggin Perry to be trustees of his estate. One of their most important duties was deciding which son, Arthur or Seth,

Billy Reed with Seth Hancock in 1973, after the younger Hancock had taken over Claiborne Farm.

would become president of Claiborne. Although Arthur was the heir apparent because he was older, the trustees picked Seth because he seemed more mature and responsible.

Deeply hurt, Arthur vowed to show the trustees that they were vastly underestimating him. He left Claiborne and started the Stone Farm next door. Over the next decade, while Seth was doing a good job of running Claiborne, Arthur slowly built his farm into one good enough to produce a Kentucky Derby winner.

Now, all these years later, here he was, the main obstacle between the Derby winner's circle and one of the men who told him he wasn't trustworthy enough to run Claiborne Farm. Although Arthur didn't talk about it publicly, he still seethed over the role Phipps had played in his life.

Interestingly, one of the horses Arthur groomed for the Phipps Stable was a mare named Marking Time. She was eventually bred to Buckpasser, who had won Horse of the Year honors for Phipps in 1966, and that mating producing a filly named Relaxing, who finished third against colts in the 1981 Jockey Club Gold Cup.

In 1985, Ogden Phipps bred Relaxing to Alydar, the brilliant Calumet Farm stallion who had finished second to Affirmed in each of the 1978 Triple Crown races. The colt, born at Claiborne on March 26, 1986, was named Easy Goer.

While Easy Goer was being raised at Claiborne, Arthur was raising Sunday Silence next door. The contrast between the two was obvious. The day he was born, Easy Goer's breeding stamped him as a potential star. But Sunday Silence was the ugly duckling that nobody wanted.

The Derby crowd made the Phipps entry of Easy Goer and stablemate Awe Inspiring the 4-to-5 favorite, and Sunday Silence the $3 to $1 second choice.

On a chilly, overcast, and wet Derby Day, the track was listed as muddy, a surface similar to the one Easy Goer had handled with pluck in the Wood Memorial.

The early pace was set by Houston, ridden by Laffit Pincay Jr. and trained by D. Wayne Lukas. But at the head of the stretch, Houston gave up the lead to Sunday Silence and jockey Pat Valenzuela. When jockey Pat Day sent Easy Goer after the leader, the Phipps colt began passing tiring horses until he was second inside the 16th pole.

But there was no catching Sunday Silence, who flashed across the finish line 2-1/2 lengths ahead of Easy Goer, who beat Awe Inspiring by only a head for second. The time for the mile and a quarter was only 2:05, the slowest Derby since Calumet's Tim Tam ran the same time in 1958.

In the aftermath, Hancock, who wore the kind of gray fedora that was in style in his father's day, was gracious toward Phipps.

"It was almost like we traded dreams," he said. "I knew he always wanted to win the Derby. I don't mean that vindictively. I hope Mr. Phipps wins the Derby next year. I like Mr. Phipps. He's been good to my family. I was bitter—hurt, really—but all things turn out for the best. It (leaving Claiborne) couldn't have turned out better for me, and it couldn't have worked out better for Claiborne."

In the Preakness, Easy Goer was favored again, but Sunday Silence took his best shot and held on for a nose victory after a fantastic stretch duel. But in the Belmont Stakes, on Easy Goer's home grounds, the Phipps colt denied Sunday Silence the Triple Crown with an eight-length victory.

The two didn't meet again until that year's Breeders Cup Classic. With Sunday Silence leading in the stretch under jockey Chris McCarron (who had replaced the suspended Valenzuela), Easy Goer uncorked a closing run that left him only a neck short.

That victory sewed up Horse of the Year honors for Sunday Silence.

After a win and a second as a 4-year-old in 1990, Sunday Silence suffered an injury that forced him to be retired to stud. Hancock wanted to stand him at Stone Farm, but couldn't find enough investors to put together a syndicate. Rather than going it alone or with only a few partners, he sold the colt to a Japanese group. Since then, Sunday Silence has been one of Japan's leading stallions.

On April 24 of this year, Ogden Phipps died at 93. He never won the Kentucky Derby.

CARL NAFZGER AND FRANCES GENTER
"I love you, Mrs. Genter!"

[From *Sports Illustrated*, February 1991]

He could easily have ended up like so many old cowboys do, wasting away in some little prairie town, living in the past and drifting, aimless as a tumbleweed. "A lot of those old cowboys just can't do it when it comes time to make the adjustment," says trainer Carl Nafzger. But he was lucky. He had the love of a good woman, a gift for working with animals and, more than anything, a desire to make sure that he wouldn't end up like the cowboys in Willie Nelson's haunting song *My Heros Have Always Been Cowboys*: the ones "sadly in search of, and one step in back of, themselves and their slow-moving dreams."

Nafzger's salvation was thoroughbred racing, a sport in which he found what he liked most about the rodeo: the freedom of life on the road and the satisfaction of figuring out what makes an animal tick. So when he married the schoolmarm, just as in those old Western matinees, Nafzger didn't ride off into the sunset. He learned and worked and improved until, last year, he arrived at the very top of the racing game.

Looking at him now, it's difficult to imagine him riding a bull, a black cowboy hat on his head, his thin body lurching this way and that as he struggles to hang on for dear life. But that was what he was—and, deep down, still is.

At 49, Nafzger is more polished, able to move easily through the elegance and sophistication of racing's upper crust. Only the twang, Texan all the way, gives him away. And maybe the hands. The big, thick hands of a man who knows what it's like to do manual labor and to make beasts, savage ones in some cases, do his bidding.

His old cowboy pals must have loved it last May 5, when he finally won the Kentucky Derby, the most famous horse race in the world. There was Nafzger, all duded up and wired for sound by ABC, calling the race for Mrs. Frances Genter, the 92-year-old pillar of the racing establishment, who had come to Churchill Downs to watch Unbridled, her first Derby starter after 50 years in the business. What happened as the splendid bay swung out of the turn for home and began moving powerfully for the lead has already become a part of racing folklore.

"He's taking the lead," Nafzger yelled to Unbridled's owner as the TV audience looked on. "He's gonna win, Mrs. Genter, he's gonna win! He's gonna win! We won it! You won the Kentucky Derby! Oh, Mrs. Genter, I love you, Mrs. Genter!"

Was that sweet or what? And the next day, with a hint of tears in his eyes, there was the old cowboy saying, "If I never win another Derby, at least I won the right one, because of Mrs. Genter." He could never show that kind of emotion at the rodeo. It would just never do, that's all, because you have to be tough and hard and mean in that rough-and-ready sport. Wanda, Carl's wife and partner, had a lot to do with teaching him something of the softer, gentler side of life.

They met in 1963, at a Denver rodeo where Carl was riding, and he became so smitten with Wanda Judson, the dark-haired, soft-spoken special education teacher, that he began writing letters to her and calling her from all the places the rodeo took him. They were married five years later, and have been a team ever since. He trains the horses; she takes care of the books. But more than that, they have hung together, comforting each other in the bad times and rejoicing quietly together when fortune smiled.

Here are Carl and Wanda for you: The night Unbridled won the Kentucky Derby, they went to a small Italian restaurant in a Louisville shopping center and, said Carl, "had some good food and a cold Heineken." And the next weekend, instead of blowing off steam in some city, they made a sentimental journey back to Arizona, back to where Carl once rode a lot of rodeo bulls and where, two decades ago, the two of them had begun campaigning horses at small tracks, those other bullrings of sport.

"Wanda and I have been real lucky," Nafzger says, thinking maybe of what might have been. "We don't have a special magic or anything. We just had a dream, and, after 22 years, we made it. But we're not going to change. I still drive the same ol' Buick and I didn't go out and buy Wanda a big diamond ring or anything. That's just not us."

One of Carl's favorite movies is *The Last Picture Show*, because it reminds him of his hometown of Olton, Texas (pop. 1,800). The closest town to Olton

Carl Nafzger and Billy Reed at Keeneland, 1997.

that anybody ever heard of is Lubbock, home of Texas Tech University and Buddy Holly. Carl liked Olton, and still does, but he also wanted to get out as soon as he could. He wanted to be somebody, to do something important, and that's hard in Olton.

His grandfather on his father's side came over from Switzerland in 1887, settled in Monroe, Wisconsin, and then moved on to Texas, where he joined the other homesteaders looking for cheap land. When Carl's father, Paul, inherited part of the family spread of about 2,000 acres, he supported his family with various kinds of farming. One year it would be cows, another year it might be turkeys or corn or cotton. But what fascinated young Carl more than anything else were the bulls. "I'd come home from school and feed the bulls," he said, "and I finally talked my dad into building me a bucking chute. He put me on my first bull, a big ol' Hereford who threw me two or three times and then sort of ran over me, too. But I loved it. From that day on, I didn't want to do anything but ride bulls. I don't know why. It became an obsession."

That obsession led him to the rodeo, which is the only place you can make money riding bulls. The deal is rather simple, really. You get on a snorting, stomping animal that weighs about 1,200 angry pounds, the chute opens and off you go. The bull tries to toss you into the next county and you try to hang on. If you stay on for eight seconds, you qualify. If you don't, you're on your butt and it's a case of better luck next time, pal. "The thing about the rodeo," Nafzger says, "is that you're completely on your own. There's nobody to buy your bus ticket for you, nobody to pick you up, nobody to cry if you break your leg."

He became a professional bull rider in 1960, a year after he graduated from high school. "Dad signed the card, and I was down the road," Carl says. From 1960 through '68, Nafzger competed on the Rodeo Cowboys Association circuit, traveling as much as 80,000 miles annually, riding a bull somewhere almost every night of the rodeo year, from the day after Christmas until early the next December. You name the stop, and Nafzger probably remembers a bull from there: Amarillo, Calgary, San Antonio, Cheyenne, Laramie. The road goes on forever when you're a rodeo cowboy.

He made $13,000 in his best year, 1963, and retired in 1968, the year he married Wanda. Then he unretired for a while, in 1969, because he and Wanda needed money for their fledgling racing operation. By the time he got off his last bull, in 1971, he had ridden more than 1,500 of the animals in about 700 different towns. He had made it to the National Finals Rodeo three times, his best finish coming in '63, when he stayed on six of his eight bulls to take third in the overall bull-riding standings.

"It takes eight seconds on the clock to ride a bull," Nafzger says, "but if you've got a bad one, it can be an eternity."

Once he caught a bad one in Wahoo, Nebraska, that slammed him against a telephone pole. Nafzger has a steel rod in his left leg to remind him of that ornery animal. He also had his nose broken five times, his teeth knocked out and numerous bones cracked. The bulls had names like Tornado and Wild Man, and Nafzger would study them until he learned their habits, their quirks. The most dangerous of them were the unpredictable ones. "I remember one out of Mesquite, Texas, that had a real rubber neck," Nafzger says. "If he ever popped you, he'd hurt you."

In the fall of 1966, Nafzger and three of his fellow cowboys were on their way to the Cow Palace in San Francisco when they decided to stop off and take a look at Keeneland racecourse in Lexington, Kentucky. Impressed by the track's stately shade trees and its emerald paddocks, Nafzger turned to his friends and said, "Boys, someday I'm going to run horses here." To which one of his friends replied, "Carl, this is the kind of place where they wouldn't let you in the grandstand."

A decade later, Carl and Wanda took some horses to Keeneland for the first time; they have been a fixture there ever since. "A lot of people in Kentucky think I've lived there all my life," says Carl.

When Carl and Wanda first met, he was a cocky 21-year-old kid who was in love with the romance of the rodeo. He thought he was pretty hot stuff, too, swaggering around in that black cowboy hat, looking a little like James Dean in *Giant*—or so some of the girls told him.

"But he had good manners, too," says Wanda. "I think that's what I liked the most about him. Also, we both liked horses. They were my hobby, and I really enjoyed them. When we got married, I didn't mind living on the road because when you have pleasure horses, like I did, you're always going to horse shows."

Carl could have taken a job in the rodeo, been an arena manager or something like that, but Wanda persuaded him to give racing a try. She sensed, maybe before he did, that he had a knack for understanding animals. "A sixth sense," says John Nerud, the respected Florida horseman who was to give Carl his first big break. At first, though, Nafzger missed the cowboy life. Still does, sometimes, except for one thing.

"Your body takes a terrible beating when you're a bull rider," says Nafzger. "It's not anything big, like a broken leg, that gets you. It's the constant pounding, night after night. After I got out of it, it was about a year before I got up one morning and felt that something was different. I finally figured out that I wasn't sore all over anymore."

The Nafzgers started at the bottom of the horse racing business in 1968 and slowly worked their way up, traveling from New Mexico to California to Louisiana, until finally they arrived in Kentucky, the mecca of the sport. While Carl worked hard at learning to translate his gift from bulls to thoroughbreds— he even took a horseshoeing course at one point—Wanda helped make ends meet by teaching school.

It was a hard life, especially in the beginning, but Carl never tired of trying to figure out the thoroughbreds. "I'm a horse psychiatrist, not a horse trainer," he likes to say. And he never lost his optimism, After a disappointment, he still says to Wanda, "We're gonna start this day all over again." In the glove compartment of the cluttered 1990 Buick Park Avenue that serves the couple as a sort of rolling office, Carl keeps a motivational tape entitled, "Be a Confident Winner."

"You have to visualize what you want to be and then be it," Nafzger constantly tells his 30 employees. "You have to review your mistakes, rerun everything you do and learn from it. I wished they'd had the video camera when I was rodeoing. I'd have been a lot better bull rider."

The break that every trainer looks for came to Nafzger in 1979, when William Floyd, an old-time Kentucky breeder, gave him a yearling colt named Fairway Phantom to train. The colt looked so promising as a 2-year-old the next year, winning the Breeders' Futurity at Keeneland and the Arch Ward Stakes in Chicago, that Carl and Wanda thought they might have their first Kentucky Derby horse. But Fairway Phantom chipped a bone in his knee and never made it to the Derby. Nevertheless, Floyd was impressed with Nafzger and recommended him to Nerud, the esteemed trainer and head of Tartan Farm in

Florida. Nerud took such a liking to the cowboy that he encouraged Mrs. Genter to give Nafzger a string of her well-bred horses to train.

"John Nerud was the first guy to put enough stock in my barn to give me a shot and, at the same time, keep the owners off my back so I could prove whether I could train or not," Nafzger says.

Even if a trainer has the gift, he can go only so far if he doesn't have the stock. Once Nafzger started getting horses with talent, his career went steadily forward. His Broken N Stable—so named because Carl was the first male Nafzger in three generations to break the tradition of staying around Olton—became a respected operation on the Florida-Kentucky-Illinois circuit in the 1980s. In 1986, he won the Breeders' Futurity at Keeneland with his 2-year-old colt Orono, beating Alysheba, who went on to win the 1987 Kentucky Derby. And he trained multiple stakes winners Smile and Star Choice for the Genter Stable.

Last year, the stable made more than $6 million, four times its previous best. Besides winning the Kentucky Derby, Unbridled came back on Oct. 27 to win the $3 million Breeders' Cup Classic at Belmont Park. And Nafzger had another nice 3-year-old, Home At Last, who won the $1 million Super Derby in Louisiana.

After the Classic, Nafzger was annoyed when the press asked him if he felt he had finally "arrived" as a trainer. Carl thought the question implied that he and Wanda had been running some kind of mom-and-pop operation that happened to get lucky. "I've been around for a while, but it's only now that anybody has started noticing," Nafzger says. "Unbridled will go someday and so will Home At Last, but we'll still be around."

He can get riled up, too. In the giddy aftermath of the Derby, while he was waiting for Mrs. Genter and her family to arrive in the Churchill Downs winner's circle, Nafzger, wearing a raincoat with an ABC sticker attached, paced restlessly, blocking some photographers' views of Unbridled and jockey Craig Perret.

"Hey, ABC," yelled one perturbed cameraman. "Get outta the way, ABC. Get down, ABC."

Eyes flashing, Nafzger spun around and shouted, "I train the son of a bitch, and we're waiting for the people who belong in here."

End of discussion. Then there was the incident before the Belmont Stakes, when Nafzger and Unbridled arrived at the Belmont Park stable area, only to find that the Kentucky Derby winner didn't have a stall.

"We finally got it worked out," he says, "but I was still fuming when I looked over at Unbridled and saw he had stretched out in the stall and gone to sleep. I thought to myself, 'Well, now we know who's got the real class in this outfit.'"

Nafzger became irritated again when, after Unbridled had finished a dull fourth in the Belmont, it was suggested that the colt had run poorly because he hadn't been given a dose of Lasix, the controversial antibleeding medication that is illegal in New York. Nafzger then swore that Unbridled would come back and prove himself on the same track in the Breeders' Cup Classic.

On that fall afternoon at Belmont, Unbridled made his trademark big kick under jockey Pat Day, split horses inside the eighth pole and drew off to a solid one-length victory. Said Nafzger, "I don't guess I'll be getting any more questions about Lasix."

♦

Last Dec. 9, a windy, overcast day in South Florida, Nafzger took Unbridled to the track between the fourth and fifth races at Calder Race Course, near Fort Lauderdale, so the colt could gallop. It was Unbridled Day at Calder, and the first 10,000 customers at the track were given free photos of the horse who won the Derby and the Classic.

The next day, Carl and Wanda took a rare afternoon off to go deep-sea fishing in the Florida Keys. On the way to the dock, Nafzger talked about how he gets the most out of a thoroughbred.

"I listen to the horse," he said. "I let him tell me what he wants to do and what he doesn't want to do, and then I adjust. Horses never make mistakes, only the people handling them do. And it's the same for just about any horse as it is with Unbridled. The development of the horse, that's the thing. A claimer can be a nice horse to watch if he's honest."

The Nafzgers arrived at Bud n' Mary's Fishing Marina, carried a big tub of fried chicken on board the Caribsea, and ordered Captain Dave Day to cast off. Half an hour later, the boat was being tossed, around by eight-foot waves, causing Nafzger to grin and yell "Whoopee!" every now and then, just as if he were riding a bull. This went on for 2-1/2 hours until finally, when one of his guests became ill, Carl reckoned it was time to get back to shore. "Motion doesn't bother me," he said. "When you're a rodeo cowboy, you learn pretty quick you're going to die."

Back on shore he signed an autograph for Captain Dave's mate and climbed into the Buick to head back home. On the way, he picked out a little tavern and pulled over to go inside and have a beer.

As he relaxed, Nafzger talked about Unbridled's past performance chart for 1990, which made the colt look sort of like a bucking bronc. Up and down. Only four wins in 11 starts. Between the Derby and the Classic, Unbridled's only victory came in a mile allowance race at Arlington Park near Chicago.

"I can't really say I blame the jockeys for any of his losses, because of my style of training," Nafzger said. "I don't lead a horse over there at the razor's edge every time. Horses can't take it, they're not machines. I had Unbridled fit and ready when he needed to be. What did the horse ever do that was bad? But a lot of the writers got mad at the horse because he wasn't unbeatable."

Still, in a year when most of the best horses were sidelined by injuries, Unbridled stayed around for the entire campaign, running his first race in January and his last in October. In his 11 starts, he never ran a really bad race. Besides his four victories, he had three seconds, two thirds, a fourth and a fifth place, for total earnings of $3.7 million. Part of Nafzger's philosophy is, "It's not how many you win, but the ones you win." By that standard, Unbridled was perfect in the two races that every horseman wants most to win—the Kentucky Derby and the Classic.

"Winning the Kentucky Derby is like being Miss America," he says, "because you become a spokesman for the game for a year." Still, Carl and Wanda are keeping it all in perspective. Nafzger remembers well when, as a young man, he had proudly showed an old cowboy a newspaper clipping that complimented his bull riding. "Carl," the old guy said, "them bulls can't read."

"When you win the Kentucky Derby, your life changes," said Nafzger, back on the road again, a tape of cowboy songs playing on the car stereo. "It makes you stop and contemplate what's really going on in your life. One day after the Derby, I looked at a picture of myself in the winner's circle and I said, 'Wanda, that's not me. . . . They're trying to make me into a horse trainer!'"

And what is he, if not that?

"A cowboy," said Carl, grinning. "I'll always be a cowboy at heart."

PAT DAY
All Good Things Come In Time

[From the *Lexington Herald-Leader*, 1991 and 1992]

A jockey gets only so many good chances to win the Kentucky Derby before his skills begin to fade and suddenly, before he knows it, the live mounts are going to younger men with quicker reflexes.

Pat Day still has time. Plenty of time. At 37, he's at the peak of his Hall of Fame career and, because of the way he takes care of himself, there's no reason to believe that he won't be at the top for another decade.

Yet his ninth-place finish Saturday aboard the long shot Corporate Report extended his record to 0-for-9 in the race every jockey wants most to win. And the maddening thing is, he could have had the mount on the victorious Strike the Gold.

It's the damnedest thing. Day owns Churchill Downs. And he has won so many important races nationally during the past decade that he's being inducted into racing's Hall of Fame this August. But the Derby continues to elude him. He is racing's Captain Ahab.

"My friends and my family are more frustrated and desirous than I am," Day said yesterday, waiting to work out Unbridled for trainer Carl Nafzger. "I desire it, but I'm not as frustrated as they are."

If so, that's as strong an advertisement for born-again Christendom as you will ever hope to find. Children of a lesser god would be driving themselves crazy at this point. But Day's serenity remains unshaken, despite the fact that he easily could be sitting on a two-race Derby winning streak right now.

Last year he won the Florida Derby on Unbridled, but surrendered the mount to Craig Perret so he could ride Summer Squall. That colt did win the Preakness, but so what? Day already had a Preakness to his credit. In the Derby, Summer Squall couldn't handle Unbridled's late charge.

This spring he was trainer Nick Zito's first choice to ride Strike the Gold. Had he wanted, he could have ridden him in the April 13 Blue Grass Stakes at Keeneland. Instead, Day and his agent, Fred Aime, opted to ride Unbridled in the Oaklawn Park Handicap.

That was a curious decision, in retrospect, because Day and Aime now have dumped Unbridled in favor of Summer Squall for Saturday's Pimlico Special. Had they committed to Squall before the Oaklawn Handicap, they would have been free to ride Strike the Gold in the Blue Grass.

So they outsmarted themselves. After the Blue Grass, instead of coming back to Day for the Derby, Zito and the colt's owners decided to stick with Chris Antley, even though he's 11 years younger than Day and not nearly as experienced in big races.

"No hard feelings," Day said yesterday. "It's hard to break up a winning combination. If it's not broke, why fix it? If Chris had stumbled or faltered in the Blue Grass, we might have got the mount. But Chris rode the horse well and got along with him and won. That's the way it goes."

Still, down deep, Day wouldn't be human if he hadn't felt as wistful after this Derby as he did when Unbridled won last year. Some years you just get beat, but others you just make the wrong moves. The wrong moves hurt the most.

Did he wish, in retrospect, that he had committed to Squall soon enough to pull out of his Oaklawn Handicap commitment to Unbridled so he could ride Strike the Gold in the Blue Grass?

"I don't think we really knew what was best at that point in time," Day said. "It was just a chain of events that occurred, and certainly we weren't in control of it. The thing about racehorses is that you never know how they'll come back after a race."

The only reason Day rode Corporate Report is that it was his only option, and his only consolation was that at least Corporate Report finished just ahead of Hansel, the post-time Derby favorite. Day also had the mount on Hansel in Florida, but dumped him to ride Richman in the Jim Beam Stakes. Yesterday Day said he thought Corporate Report ran an encouraging race in the Derby, considering his relative lack of seasoning, and he was pleased to hear that trainer D. Wayne Lukas intends to give him another chance in the May 18 Preakness.

"He got awful tired on me at the eighth pole," Day said.

You can't blame a top jockey and his agent for wanting to ride as many of the best horses as possible. Yet sometimes, by trying to ride too many at once, they can get themselves trapped in conflicts that only create tension and resentment among the trainers for whom they work.

At this point in his career, considering how much Day wants to win the Derby, he and Aime should put that above all else. Beginning now, their No. 1 priority should be doing everything humanly possible to make certain that Day is on a strong contender in next year's Derby.

The clock is ticking on Day's career. Nothing to panic about, understand, but it's also true that he can't afford to make many more unlucky choices. Sure, Bill Shoemaker won the Derby when he was 54, but that was an aberration. And, sure, Angel Cordero Jr., who's 48, had a mount in this year's Derby. But Cordero, who has won the roses three times, was able to get only the long shot Qintana. He doesn't have the choices he had 10 years ago.

If Day ever thinks about any of this, he never lets on. Only the stubborn glint in his eyes belies the philosophical calm in his voice.

"All good things," he said, "come in time."

✦

[Day won the 1992 Kentucky Derby aboard Lil E. Tee.]

For a guy who didn't get much sleep, who said he "tore the bed up" because of the adrenaline rush he got from finally winning the Kentucky Derby, Pat Day was in a pretty playful mood when he arrived at Churchill Downs yesterday morning.

The jockey sneaked up behind Lynn Whiting and put his hands over the trainer's eyes, making him guess who was the latest person to come by Barn 18 and offer congratulations.

When Whiting gave up and turned around, a laughing Day said, "How'd you make the evening? Your eyes are still bright. How's 'E.T.' doing?"

Whiting assured him that Lil E. Tee, the colt who gave Day his first Derby win in his 10th attempt, was doing fine and probably would be pointed for the May 14 Preakness, the second jewel in racing's Triple Crown.

And so it went yesterday morning as the home team—Whiting, Day and owner Cal Partee have been Churchill Downs regulars for years—celebrated the biggest win of their careers.

Sent off at 16–1 odds, Lil E. Tee made Derby history by looking the ballyhooed Arazi in the eye and drawing away from him to win the 118th Run for the Roses.

An Arab oil sheik paid $9 million for half of Arazi, which only proves again that you can't buy a place in posterity. When it was all over, the Derby belonged to the folks who had spent a good portion of their careers laboring in the shadows of Churchill's twin spires.

Jockey Pat Day won his first Kentucky Derby in 1992 with Lil E. Tee.

Talking yesterday morning with reporters, Whiting was interrupted regularly by the exercise riders, grooms and hotwalkers who will be with him long after the Derby media horde is gone. They all were happy. They all were glad to see hard work rewarded.

Yet thrilled and excited as they were for Whiting and Partee, they were especially pleased for Day.

The holder of most of the track's riding records, Day had somehow managed to miss the biggest race of all, mostly because of bad racing luck.

He has ridden favorites who bled and had to be pulled up (Demons Begone, 1987), hyped horses who didn't like the track (Easy Goer, 1989) and contenders who didn't get a break (Rampage, 1986).

But this time Day enjoyed both a perfect trip and a break. A lot of observers will tell you that had A.P. Indy been able to run (he was scratched on Saturday morning because of a leg injury), he would have won easily.

So how big a day was Saturday for Pat?

"I don't believe anybody on God's green earth deserves the joy I'm feeling right now," Day said yesterday morning. "But I'm glad I was able to taste it. The longer you wait, the sweeter it tastes."

Whiting celebrated by going to dinner at the restaurant Hasenour's. He received a standing ovation when he walked in.

But Day, ever humble, went home to be with friends. On the way out of the track, however, he stopped to visit Lil E. Tee, who was so engrossed in his feed tub that he barely paused to accept the peppermint Day gave him.

Later, a huge surprise awaited the jockey at his home in the eastern part of Jefferson County.

"I told one of my neighbors," Day said, "that if I won the Derby, you'd have to use a butterfly net to catch me. When I got home, a butterfly net was on the front door."

Maybe he should have sent the net to Francois Boutin, the trainer of Arazi who left Louisville pointing fingers at the colt's co-owners for forcing him to run Arazi in a race that he didn't like.

Now, while Arazi is shipped back to Europe, Lil E. Tee apparently will go for the American Triple Crown. The only question now is this: Is he really a superb colt, or was yesterday's race just a fluke?

To Pat Day, it makes no difference. "Derby week wears you out," Whiting told him yesterday.

"Yeah," Day said, "but it's so sweet when you win it that the sweetness overcomes all that."

MIKE BARRY
The World's Greatest Handicapper

[From the Kentucky Derby program, 1992]

There's never been a sportswriter who loved the Kentucky Derby quite like Mike Barry did. He loved to look forward to it, to write about it, to view it, to assign each one a special niche in his memory. In the weeks leading up to the Derby, he would even fret about the weather. He wanted the arrival of the Derby and the blooming of the spring flowers to coincide, just so visitors could see Louisville at its best.

"When the flowers are out," he would say, "there's no prettier place in the world than Louisville at Derby time."

That might sound strange, coming from a sportswriter who, during his fifty-something-year career with the feisty little *Kentucky Irish American* and the powerful *Courier-Journal* and *Louisville Times*, gained the reputation of a wise guy. He was certainly that, often getting a rise from the pompous, the vain, and the foolish with the needle he wielded so deftly, but he was more. At heart Mike was truly an Irishman, sentimental to the core and a firm believer that laughter was the best way to cope when life dealt you a bad hand or an unplayable lie.

He was 82 going on 28 when cancer finally got the better of him in the wee hours of Friday, January 10. He died peacefully at his home in Louisville's Highlands, with his wife, Bennie, and all of his seven children nearby. Until the end, he was the youngest old man anybody ever knew. His wife said it best. "When I married Mike," Bennie said, "he was a brash young man. Now he's a brash old man." They would have been married 46 years on January 17, a week after he died.

I'll venture to say that in Louisville's neighborhood taverns and bowling alleys and pool halls, Mike was easily the most popular sportswriter ever to turn a phrase. That's because he understood the feelings and frustrations of Joe Fan. Although he had a marvelous vocabulary and command of the language, he never wrote down to his audience. "Keep it simple," he always said. "Speak the language of the common guy. And whatever else you do, never be dull." To Mike, dullness was journalism's unpardonable sin.

Just about anybody could read Mike Barry and see a bit of himself. As a golfer, Mike was "a dogged victim of inexorable fate," to borrow Dan Jenkins' line. As a horse player, he was self-styled "world's greatest handicapper," as anyone could easily tell by noticing the photo of himself that he always ran with his sports column in the *Kentucky Irish American*—the one where you could see the hole in the sole of his shoe. And as a fan, he couldn't abide fat-headed owners, overpaid players, win-at-any-cost coaches, or big-mouthed announcers.

He and I had some fierce arguments about sports. I thought Pete Rose was a terrific baseball player, and Mike thought he was overrated. I gave A.B. "Happy" Chandler a lot of credit for helping Jackie Robinson break baseball's color barrier in 1948, and Mike thought Chandler didn't deserve it. I admired Muhammad Ali for having the courage of his convictions, and Mike thought he was a draft-dodger. And so on. Yet, for all our bickering, we never had a harsh word. We both understood that differences of opinion are what make the sports world turn.

To be honest, I often envied Mike for living in a world where everything was black or white. In my years as a columnist, I've often gotten bogged down in grays. But to Mike, everything was either this way or that. Period. And once he took a stand, he would never change his mind, new information to the contrary notwithstanding. But right or wrong, Mike was going to do it louder, and with more flair, than anybody. Just ask anybody who ever hung out with him at the old S&H bar downtown or the Bambi bar on Bardstown Road.

Mike loved golf, basketball, football and baseball. He tolerated tennis, but had no use for soccer, polo or any sport where you have to get cold to do it. In golf, he loved Arnold Palmer and rooted for our local pros, especially Fuzzy Zoeller of New Albany and Jodie Mudd of Louisville. In baseball and football, his favorites were U of L and Notre Dame, especially when they were playing "The Big Blew," which is how he referred to Kentucky and its fans. In baseball, he liked the Boston Red Sox, which was the parent club most of the time when Louisville's Triple-A team was the Colonels, and anybody who was playing the Cincinnati Reds. One of his pet peeves was Louisville writers and broadcasters who called the Cincinnati team "our Reds."

But the Derby was his favorite. He saw just about every one since 1922, missing only a few during World War II when he was serving with the U.S. Army in the Pacific, He always took it upon himself to serve as sort of unofficial host for the out-of-town Derby writers, wandering the press box to answer questions about past Derbys, find newcomers who needed help, and, naturally, offer his opinion to anyone who cared to listen. Bill Hennessy, his cousin and close friend, remembers that when the weather turned cold just before the 1957 Derby, Mike rounded up a bunch of coats for writers who might have come to town without them.

His favorite Derby winner was Citation, Calumet Farm's Triple Crown champion of 1948, and it always irked him when younger writers insisted that Secretariat was the greatest thoroughbred ever. "Secretariat was a good horse," Mike would say, "but Citation could beat him pulling a wagon." Did I mention that Mike was apt to occasionally engage in a little hyperbole? Of the champions of more recent vintage, Mike liked 1977 Triple Crown winner Seattle Slew and his trainer, Billy Turner.

At least Mike bowed out a winner. When we went to the 1991 Florida Derby, Mike picked up on a colt named Strike the Gold, a fast-closing second that day to winter-book favorite Fly So Free. A subsequent victory over Fly So Free in Keeneland's Blue Grass Stakes made Strike the Gold Mike's Derby horse. Last Derby Week he carried around the front-page of *The Voice-Tribune* of St. Matthews, which had printed Mike's Derby predictions under this World War III headline: "Mike Barry Picks Strike the Gold." A couple of days after the

Mike Barry and Nick Zito with the front page of The Voice-Tribune.

Derby, I took Mike out to Churchill so he and Nick Zito, Strike the Gold's trainer, could pose together holding up the paper's front page.

Before they closed his casket, per his request, they put in the ancient putter (circa 1910) that Mike used in every round of golf he ever played. It was a homely device—our friend Dave Kindred once wrote that it had to be a curtain rod in a previous existence—but Mike loved it dearly, no matter how often it betrayed him.

He also left us laughing. When he instructed his daughter Julie that he wanted his casket closed for the funeral-home visitation, he also told her to put this caption under the photo that was placed atop it: "And this was going to be the year I won the Masters."

Maybe this was also going to be the year when he picked another Derby winner. The flowers my wife and I sent to the funeral home were red roses. Kentucky Derby roses. I thought Mike would appreciate that, considering how much he cared about what happened in Louisville on the first Saturday in May.

✦

Barry saw 66 runnings of the Churchill Downs classic, and he had an opinion on many of the starters. First with the *Kentucky Irish American*, later with *The Louisville Times* and then in retirement with *The Voice-Tribune*, he produced these pre-race comments:

• Northern Dancer (1964)— "This horse never runs any bad races. The only argument seems to be about how good some of his races are. I expect him to run another good race Saturday, to be out of trouble with his speed, and to win the Derby." [Note: Mike was right on the money. Not only did Northern Dancer win the Derby, but he set a track record of two minutes flat.]

• Dawn Glory (1967) — "There isn't a horse in Puerto Rico that can beat him. Saturday's race won't be in Puerto Rico."

• Our Trade Winds (1972)— "This one will be running at the end. The end of the day, that is."

• Shamgo (1979) — "His trainer says he can run all day. That's just how much time he needs—starting late in the afternoon, he's dead."

• Bold 'n Ruling (1980) — "This is one of those horses who can run all day. Unfortunately, all day won't be enough time for him to finish a mile and a quarter. You've got to be discouraged when you see his jockey leave the paddock wearing a miner's helmet and carrying sandwiches." [Bold 'n Ruling started the race on May 3, 1980, and finished it on May 3, 1980, but he came in sixth at 68-1 odds, was injured in the race and never started again. Sandwiches, anyone?]

• Gato Del Sol (1982) — "This means something like 'Cat of the Sun.' It also means the sun may set before he finishes." [Note: Let's see now . . . The horses were off and running in the 1982 Derby at 5:40. Gato Del Sol took two minutes and 2-2/5 seconds to win the race. Sunset was at 8:34 that day. So that means Mike was off by a mere 2 hours and 52 minutes. Oh well, nobody's perfect.]

• Slew o' Gold (1983) — "Bet all the money you've got on this one—all the Confederate money, all the Monopoly money, all the Pitcairn Island money..."

• Fali Time (1984) — "As good as anything in California. This year, that's like saying you can't find a better figure skater in Saudi Arabia."

• Pendleton Ridge (1990) — "This maiden closed well to be fourth in the Wood. No maiden has won the Derby in 57 years. After Saturday it'll be 58."

• Green Alligator (1991) — "Supposed to have gotten his name from an Irish song. I've been to a lot of Irish parties, but no one ever reached the stage where anybody was singing about green alligators. Even if they saw some."

WILLIAM T. YOUNG
The Classiest Act

[From the *Lexington Herald-Leader,* May 1996]

The snowy-haired gentleman—a term, by the way that fits William T. Young as snugly as his business suits—wasn't about to leave his box seat at Churchill Downs until the victory was certain.

This was the Kentucky Derby, the race the 78-year-old Young always has coveted more than most because he's Bluegrass to his very core, and the finish had been a blur of sound and fury, too close to call,

Young thought—wished, hoped, prayed, if you will—that Grindstone, his handsome son of 1990 Derby winner Unbridled, had collared Cavonnier right at the wire.

But he wasn't about to start moving until the numbers went up on the tote board. He learned that lesson in 1985, on a wintry November afternoon at Aqueduct, when he was certain that his Storm Cat had won the Breeders' Cup Juvenile.

Giddy with joy, Young and his friends took off for the winner's circle, only to learn upon their arrival that a colt named Tasso had gotten up to nose out Storm Cat.

Embarrassed, Young promised himself that he would never again head for a winner's circle until the result was official.

So yesterday he sat there, preparing himself to deal with either his biggest thrill in racing or his most bitter defeat.

The seconds seemed like minutes, the minutes like hours.

W.T. Young's Grindstone wins the 1996 Kentucky Derby for Overbrook Farm.

Finally, there were the numbers, glowing in the hazy Louisville afternoon.

On top was No. 4, Grindstone, who had been considered the lesser half, behind Editor's Note, of the Young entry trained by D. Wayne Lukas.

And at this auspicious moment, the crowning glory of his career as a horseman and a Kentuckian, this is what William T. Young said: "Oh, boy."

No theatrics, no fist-pumping, no gloating. Just "Oh, boy." This is why words such as "courtly" and "genteel" and "classy" always come to mind when somebody mentions Young.

When John Y. Brown, Jr. was governor of Kentucky, he persuaded Young to join his cabinet—at the grand salary of $1 a year—because, said Brown,

"He's the brightest person I've ever known."

To appreciate that, of course, you have to be around Young for a while. You have to cut through all that modesty and all that self-deprecating humor. The next time Young toots his own horn, it will be the first time.

At first blush, Young and Lukas would seem to be racing's oddest couple. Young is modest to a fault, a trait that nobody has ever attributed to Lukas.

Where Lukas needs the spotlight like Geraldo needs a daily O.J. fix, Young prefers to stay behind the scenes. Many times during their relationship, Young has cringed at some outrageous Lukas observation or prediction.

But, really, they're incredibly alike. Both are self-made men who used their brains and their relentless work ethics to become successful beyond their wildest dreams.

In addition, both are businessmen first and foremost.

Young hooked up with Lukas for a very pragmatic reason: Lukas knows how to win races and earn money.

"He appeared to me to be a winner," Young said.

The foundation of Young's fortune was peanut butter. He marketed a brand, Big Top, that he sold to Procter & Gamble for beaucoup bucks.

You can see Lukas, in a different time and place, selling peanut butter, can't you? Sure you can.

"We're oriented the same way," Young said.

If the measure of a person is not how much money he makes, but how

W.T. Young and Billy Reed

107

he uses it, Young deserves a place in the Philanthropy Hall of Fame.

Who knows how many good people and good causes he has helped? At Transylvania University, one of his most important projects, he's regarded as virtually a saint.

And then there's the University of Kentucky library fund drive and heaven only knows what else. He has used his money generously and wisely. The next time you're looking about for examples of a life well-lived, remember William T. Young.

The best thing he said in his post-race press conference was this: "If you don't have friends, winning the Kentucky Derby doesn't mean much."

In 1992, friendship was the reason Young purchased an Unbridled breeding season that the Frances Genter estate had donated to the Derby Museum.

His buddy Carl Pollard, one of the museum's leading patrons, was afraid the season wouldn't bring enough at auction to help the museum.

"Some people thought it might be worth no more than $15,000," said Young, who coughed up $30,000 without blinking.

His breeding experts took the Unbridled season and decided to mate the Derby winner with the mare Buzz My Bell. Who could have guessed the result would be the 1996 Derby winner?

And then there was the steadfast way that Young stuck by Lukas after the 1993 Preakness, when Union City—a colt owned by Young and trained by Lukas—broke a leg and had to be humanely destroyed.

At that point Lukas' critics in the media wrote his obituary.

A couple said he never again would be an important player on the national stage because he had been exposed as a horseman who had far more ego than horse sense.

Had Young pushed the panic button and given his horses to another trainer, Lukas, indeed, might never have recovered. But Young hung tough. He never flinched.

And so here he was late yesterday afternoon, saying this as he basked in the afterglow of the victory he wanted most: "I think that when you give, you probably get twice back."

At least, sometimes, you get what you deserve, even if you have to wait a few extra anxious moments before you learn that it's real.

Oh, boy.

LUKAS, BAFFERT AND ZITO
We Three Kings

[From the *Lexington Herald-Leader*, April 1999]

We might as well call them the "Three Amigos" because they are about as friendly toward each other as three driven, competitive, proud trainers can be in their relentless pursuit of the Kentucky Derby, the most popular and coveted thoroughbred race in the world.

Bob Baffert, D. Wayne Lukas and Nick Zito are entirely different in approach, personality and style. Yet they are destined to be tied together in Derby history because each has won the roses twice in this decade, the first time this century that such a thing has happened.

So Saturday's 125th Derby will have a special meaning for them. Baffert, who won the Derby in 1997 with Silver Charm and last year with Real Quiet, will be attempting to become the first trainer to win the roses three consecutive years.

The Baffert contingent will be formidable. The huge gelding General Challenge won the Santa Anita Derby, and the colt Prime Timber was runner-up. They figure to be the top two choices in the Derby's morning line, unless Baffert also enters either Silverbulletday or Excellent Meeting, his wondrous fillies who can run in either the Derby or the Kentucky Oaks on Friday.

But Lukas and Zito are standing squarely in his way with entries that could derail the Baffert Express and allow one of them to lay claim to the title of "Derby Trainer of the Decade."

Lukas, whose three Derby victories include Thunder Gulch in 1995 and Grindstone a year later, will come at Baffert with Cat Thief, a solid contender all spring in some of the toughest Derby prep races, and Charismatic, a late-blooming colt who was impressive in winning the Coolmore Lexington Stakes at Keeneland on April 18.

Billy Reed with Nick Zito..

Zito, who won the Derby in 1991 with Strike the Gold and in 1994 with Go for Gin, has high hopes for Stephen Got Even and Adonis, the winners of Turfway Park's major Derby prep and the Wood Memorial, respectively, in their most recent outings.

"I like Nick," says Baffert. "I respect him. When he shows up with a good horse, he's always a threat. As for Lukas, I've learned from him. I've watched how he deals with horses and with people. He's helped me learn what to do and what not to do."

Baffert and Zito had quicker success in the Derby than Lukas, who needed seven appearances and 12 entrants before he finally won the roses with the roan filly Winning Colors in 1988.

Zito, 51, first came to the Derby in 1990 with Thirty Six Red, the winner of the Wood Memorial. That colt finished up the track, but Zito became so enamored with the experience that—just as Lukas had done in 1981—he set the Derby as his No. 1 goal.

And doggoned if he didn't win the roses in 1991, only his second attempt, when Strike the Gold came from off the pace to win the mile-and-a-quarter classic while Zito, who was wired for TV, shouted, "Show me the way . . . show me the way!"

After missing the Derby for two years, Zito returned and won again in 1994 with Go for Gin, who found the sloppy Churchill Downs track to his liking. Second in that Derby was Strode's Creek, who was trained by Charlie Whittingham, the legendary California-based trainer who died last week at 86. "He came over to me the day after the Derby," Zito said, "and he called me his 'nice little Italian boy from New York.' They took a picture of us that I kept for years. The one thing about Charlie Whittingham that I noticed was that when the chips were down, he delivered." Just as University of Kentucky basketball fans became enamored with Rick Pitino, an Italian-American coach from New York, so have many Derby fans fallen in love with Zito, who professes his love for Kentucky, Louisville and Wagner's Pharmacy (the legendary breakfast spot across from the track) at every opportunity.

But when it comes to clothes, Pitino, who favors Armani suits, has more in common with the stylish Lukas than with Zito, who trains horses for him in the name of Celtic Pride Stable. Success has not changed Zito, a New York street guy who's most comfortable in his work clothes.

"I think the average person relates to me," Zito says. "Baffert's claim to fame is that he's very loose. That's one of his great traits, and come Derby time, that really helps.

"Lukas is a very effective person. His whole demeanor, no matter how you look at it, is very impressive. His recruiting skills are beyond belief. Every time you look around, he's got a new owner. He's unchallenged in that regard."

But Zito is being modest. Last year, after Texas furniture mogul James "Mattress Mac" MacIngvale got angry and pulled 15 horses from him, Zito regrouped and still finished fourth in the Derby with Halory Hunter, a colt owned by Pitino's group.

D. Wayne Lukas and Billy Reed.

The truth be told, Zito is sort of the odd man out in the Three Amigos. He spends a lot of time knocking on wood for luck and talking about how blessed he has been. He seems to fret about things more than Baffert and Lukas, who do a better job of hiding their insecurities. Zito liked it when a TV reporter referred to him as a "tortured soul."

Unlike Zito, who's been a thoroughbred guy from the time he used to sneak into Aqueduct racetrack in his native Queens, both Baffert and Lukas come from quarter-horse backgrounds, and both aspire to dominate the sport nationally in a way that Zito doesn't.

Since bursting on to the national scene when Codex won the 1980 Pieakness, Lukas, 63, has set standards for wins and earnings that will never be matched. His appetite for success is insatiable. It's gotten to the point where it seems almost strange if there's a graded stakes race anywhere that doesn't have a horse wearing one of Lukas' trademark white bridles.

Lukas' critics, of which he has many, accuse him of coveting the big events so avidly that he breaks down a lot more horses than, say, trainers such as Bill Mott and Richard Mandella, who concentrate on the big events for older horses.

But Lukas' counter-argument is that he wants to win the high-profile races that matter the most. In an incredible three-year stretch from the 1994 Preakness through the 1996 Belmont, he won seven of eight Triple Crown races.

Jan Reed, Susan Reed Kosko, Billy Reed, Bob Baffert, and Rob Frederick.

"There are a lot of ways to approach this game and still be successful," Lukas says. "I always watch what the other guy is doing, but I'm more convinced than ever that there's no set pattern to winning these things, no how-to book."

Whatever Baffert is doing, it's working incredibly well. No trainer in Derby history has had such an impact on the race so quickly. Had Cavonnier not lost a photo finish to the Lukas-trained Grindstone in 1996, Baffert, the youngest Amigo at 46, right now could be shooting for his fourth consecutive victory.

"The Derby, I never dreamed about being in this position until I came here with Cavonnier," Baffert said. "You always think about it, but unless you get lucky or stumble on a horse, you don't actually think it can happen. This is the first year when I've actually had the money behind me to find something (at the yearling sales)."

Silver Charm's owners, Bob and Beverly Lewis, were introduced to the sport by Lukas. They're the owners of Charismatic, and the competitor in Lukas would no doubt find it especially sweet to end Baffert's run with horse owned by the Lewises.

Mike Pegram, owner of Real Quiet and Silverbulletday, had much to do with talking Baffert into giving up the quarter horses and training thoroughbreds fulltime. Among the more recent additions to Baffert's list of clients are Aaron U. Jones, owner of Prime Timber, and John Mabee of Golden Eagle Farms, owner of General Challenge.

Both are in their twilight years and both have never won the Derby. By hopping on the Baffert bandwagon, they're hoping to win the Derby while they are still active enough to enjoy it.

Every year, the media circus around Baffert has grown more frenzied, which is what he gets for being so friendly and quotable. Yet now it seems as if he doesn't quite enjoy it as much as he did at first. The limelight is fine, so long as it doesn't interfere with the most important job—getting a horse ready to win the Kentucky Derby.

"When I came in here with Cavonnier," Baffert said, "I talked to maybe two guys from the media. I thought, 'Where's the coverage? I need some coverage.' But now it's like I'm Dennis Rodman. Everything I do is scrutinized. If I win another Derby, I'm eligible for the National Enquirer."

"It can get so demanding that you get to the point where you feel like blowing up, like Lukas did a couple of years ago. I hope I don't do that, but I can understand it. I want to promote the sport, we all do, but sometimes I wish I could just sort of hide in my tack room and train my horses."

The other two Amigos would understand better than anyone.

[Epilogue: Charismatic won the 1999 Derby for Lukas, and Baffert won the 2002 classic with War Emblem. Heading into the 2003 Derby, the score is Lukas 4, Baffert 3, Zito 2.]

BOB AND BEVERLY LEWIS
The Ozzie and Harriet of Racing

[From the *Lexington Herald-Leader,* June 1999]

On the surface, Bob and Beverly Lewis almost seem like TV sitcom characters, the modern-day Ozzie & Harriet of thoroughbred racing. He's the gentleman with the basso profundo who's always talking about how wonderful it is to be part of the great sport of thoroughbred racing. She's the dutiful wife, smiling and nodding and speaking only when prodded.

Yet there's more than meets the eye with racing's first couple, even though what meets the eye is pleasant and charming. They came up the hard way, Bob using his wits and work ethic and salesmanship to rise from beer-truck driver to the head of a multi-million-dollar beer distributorship in California. "Quite frankly," Bob Lewis said yesterday, "we worked our butts off."

So here they are now, in their twilight years, poised on the brink of immortality in a sport that Bob, 75, has loved since his parents first took him to Santa Anita in 1934. On Saturday, their Charismatic will attempt to achieve what barely eluded their Silver Charm in 1997—a victory in the Belmont Stakes that would make him racing's 12th Triple Crown winner and the first since Affirmed in 1978.

But don't make the mistake of thinking this opportunity is something the Lewises just fell into. To the contrary, the Charismatic story is a classic example of the toughness and guts and intuition that enabled the Lewises to realize The Great American Success Story in the beer industry.

In November, 1996, on advice of trainer Ray Bell, Lewis handed Tom

114

Bob and Beverly Lewis at Churchill Downs.

Roach, the co-breeder of Charismatic, a check for $200,000 in a private transaction. At the time, Charismatic was a weanling.

The plan was for Ray Bell to train the colt for the Lewises. However, unfortunately for Ray, Bob Lewis got into a business dispute with Bell's father, Tom, who was then working as a bloodstock agent.

Lewis said it had something to do with the fact that the elder Bell was trying to sell a Lewis-owned horse for twice the price that had been authorized by Lewis.

At any rate, Lewis was so "disturbed," as he puts it, that he gave Ray Bell an either/or choice—keep Charismatic or keep his dad as a part of his operation. One or the other. It was his steeliness, his sense of propriety, coming out.

"I'm a competitive-type guy and a sales person," Lewis said "Do I get hard-nosed on occasion? Yes, I do. I want to have a good chemistry with the people I work with."

When Ray Bell said he had to stick with his father, Lewis understood. But that also meant that he was going to move Charismatic and another yearling, Star Sprint, to either D. Wayne Lukas or Bob Baffert.

He picked Lukas.

"I don't know why," Lewis said. "I just made a decision and it seemed appropriate at the time. But I could have sent him to Baffert. Yes, that's exactly right."

"Bob called me," Lukas said, "and said he had two horses he wanted me to have. He said they were over at Ray Bell's barn. I saw Ray on the track and said, 'Did Bob call you?' When he said yes, I sent over a couple of grooms to pick them up."

At the time, of course, Lukas was on a roll in which he had won seven of the previous eight Triple Crown races. But later that year, rising-star Baffert made the Lewises household names in the racing industry by falling just short of the Triple Crown with their Silver Charm.

Lewis' second big decision with Charismatic came after the chestnut colt seemed destined to be just another plodder. Hoping to cut his losses, he twice authorized Lukas to put him in a $62,500 claiming race. But when there were no takers, Lukas redoubled his efforts toward trying to figure out the colt. The rest, as they say, is history.

After Charismatic's wins in the Kentucky Derby and Preakness, Bob and Beverly did their usual "America is a great country" routine.

But when Baffert seemed to imply that his filly Silverbulletday was the best 3-year-old in the country and that he wouldn't run her in the Belmont because he "didn't want to rain on their parade," Lewis reacted with a vehemence that seemed uncharacteristic.

He offered to bet Baffert $100,000 that Charismatic would finish ahead of Silverbulletday in the Belmont, with the winner donating the money to a charity of his choice.

Even more intriguing, he also said he might have to take Baffert "to the woodshed," and that Baffert's remarks were "typical of the Baffert humor, which is getting a little old."

Lukas, for one, wasn't surprised.

"He's really competitive and proud," Lukas said. "You throw a few barbs out and he'll test you. He's too classy to call you a cockroach, but he's got some fire to him."

So racing finally got to see the other side of Lewis. The side that, in the 1950s, made him gamble to cast his lot with Anheuser-Busch, then far from a sure thing in the brewing industry. The side that had made a lot of tough calls when it came to firing employees.

In other words, Bob Lewis did not build the Foothill Beverage Company into one that sells 10 million cases of beer per year by being only the affable Mr. Nice Guy that America sees on the presentation stands, smiling and waggling his latest trophy and sweetly asking his bride of 51 years to express her feelings. "I don't seem to have a conflict with decision making," Lewis said.

Win or lose, the Lewises already have scheduled a party for Saturday night at the Garden City Hotel. One thing that has endeared them to the racing world is their class. When they lose, it's with dignity and grace. When they win, it's with ebullience tempered by humility.

"I'm really happy to be in this position with the Lewises," Lukas said. "To have two chances at this thing in three years is amazing. I'm extremely happy to give the Lewises that opportunity that escaped them before."

If you want to translate that to mean that Lukas would dearly love to give the Lewises something that Baffert couldn't, help yourself. But Lewis said that even if Baffert spoils Charismatic's Triple Crown bid with Silverbulletday, there'll be no hard feelings.

"If they feel they're qualified to be here, then I hope they're here," Lewis said. "The more the merrier. But on Monday, everything goes back to normal and we can all begin looking forward to who knows what."

[Epilogue: Charismatic looked like a winner in the Belmont, but suffered a leg injury in the stretch that made him lucky to be third. Just past the finish, jockey Chris Antley pulled him up, jumped off, and held the colt's injured foreleg until medical help arrived. Although Charismatic never ran again, Antley's actions may have saved his life.]

JOHN AND DONNA WARD
A Family Affair

[From the *Lexington Herald-Leader*, May 2001]

Weep no more, my lady. Sing one song for our old Kentucky home. Lift a mint julep in tribute to John T. Ward, Jr., the winning trainer in the 127th Kentucky Derby, a native son who's a Bluegrass hardboot from the top of his unruly mop of blond-gray hair to the bottom of his soul.

You might think this sort of thing happens all the time in the world's most coveted race, given that the Lexington area has long been home to champion thoroughbreds and immortal horsemen.

Yet you would be wrong. In the last half-century, the Derby has been won by trainers from Canada, Argentina, Venezuela and Puerto Rico. It has been won by trainers based in New York, California, and Florida.

Even the native Kentuckians who have won it, gifted horsemen such as Woody Stephens and Mack Miller, had forsaken the Bluegrass to seek their fortunes in New York. But now, finally, the roses have been won by a Kentuckian whose farm is just across Rice Road from Keeneland.

On an insufferably steamy afternoon at Churchill Downs, the gray colt Monarchos came from 13th place to beat 16 rivals in what was touted as one of the deepest and most talented Derby fields ever.

The margin of victory was 4-3/4 lengths, the largest gap since Spend a Buck won by 5-1/4 lengths in 1985. Like Spend a Buck, Monarchos benefited from a track so fast that three records were set in yesterday's preliminary races. His time for the mile-and-a-quarter was 1:59.97. Only Secretariat's 1:59-2/5 in

Billy Reed with Donna Ward.

1973 was a faster winning time. The pace was so fast that it set things up perfectly for Monarchos' trademark late kick.

"When I saw the fractions, I knew we were home," Ward said. "That pace had to fry the rest of the field just when my horse was getting to the part of the racetrack that he likes best."

That, of course, would be the stretch. While the front-runners were getting wobbly, Monarchos unleashed a surge of power that caused him to have a close encounter of some kind with the long shot Invisible Ink, who finished second.

John Velasquez, the rider of Invisible Ink, lodged a bogus foul claim that the stewards, to their credit, recognized for what it was. After reviewing the replays and interviewing both riders, they declared the race official, causing Ward to raise a fist in celebration as he headed for the winner's circle.

The victory was a tribute to jockey Jorge Chavez, who won his first Derby; owners John and Debby Oxley, who have provided Ward and his wife, Donna, with the backing necessary to buy and train top-quality horses; and breeder Jim Squires.

But mostly it was a tribute to Ward's horsemanship. When he proudly said that he trained Monarchos "the old-fashioned way," he was paying homage to all the Kentucky trainers who taught him that the horse always comes before ambition and that patience is the most important of all virtues.

Yesterday Ward said that Stephens, who won the Derby with Cannonade in 1974 and Swale 10 years later, was "like an uncle to me." One of his real uncles, Sherrill, finished fourth in Secretariat's Derby with Forego, who went on to become a two-time Horse of the Year.

On the day he won the Derby, he didn't forget his predecessors.

"I grew up around some of the great older trainers in the game," he said. "They always taught me that, if you take care of the horse, the horse will take care of you."

In the early 1990s, Ward agreed to temporarily take charge of Calumet Farm at a time when that Kentucky shrine was in terrible financial shape. He did his best to deal with the farm's creditors.

When Henryk de Kwiatkowski eventually came riding in on his white horse to save the ranch, Ward quietly faded into the background, only to emerge in a new and different way when he and Donna hooked up with the Oxleys, the owners of their dreams.

When their filly, Beautiful Pleasure, became a champion two years ago, Ward refused to take much of the credit. Instead, he repeatedly told reporters that, although his name was in the program, his wife was really the filly's trainer. Imagine that. A self-effacing trainer in a cutthroat business dominated by huge egos. In that respect, he's much like Tom Hammond, the Lexington native and resident who yesterday realized a lifelong dream by playing host to NBC's first Derby telecast.

While not the sort to brag, Ward's confidence in Monarchos was as unshakeable as his game plan was flawless. The colt won the Florida Derby with a breathtaking move in the turn for home.

Then Ward brought him to Churchill, to get him acclimated, before shipping him to New York for the Wood Memorial, where he finished second to Congaree.

"I kept telling you guys that he had a big chance and I got away with it," Ward said. "You can really embarrass yourself like that."

Then he laughed the soft, gentle laugh of a Kentuckian who had come to Churchill Downs on the first Saturday in May and walked away with the prize of his childhood dreams.